Pierre-Paul Gruel Self-Portrait 1825

FRENCH
BOOKBINDERS

1789—1848

FRENCH

BOOKBINDERS

1789—1848

By

CHARLES
RAMSDEN

LONDON

B. T. BATSFORD LTD

© *Charles Ramsden 1950*
First published 1950
Reprinted 1989

ISBN 0 7134 6416 X

PRINTED AND BOUND IN GREAT BRITAIN BY
COURIER INTERNATIONAL LTD, TIPTREE, ESSEX
FOR THE PUBLISHERS
B. T. BATSFORD LTD
4 FITZHARDINGE STREET, LONDON, W1H 0AH

CONTENTS

ACKNOWLEDGEMENTS

This part of an author's task, when his work has been largely one of compilation, is perhaps one of the most difficult. I am, in my case, very fully conscious not only of my indebtedness, but even more of the fact that without the help which I have received this work would have been far less complete than it actually is.

Personally I can say that I have received help from so many institutions and persons that I find the task of acknowledging their individual contributions rendered difficult by a fear of making invidious distinctions. Fundamentally, I feel equally grateful to an unknown correspondent who has provided me with one small particle of information on a single binder as to the librarian of a French provincial library, who has furnished me with details of some twenty or more binders covering the whole period with which I am endeavouring to deal. I therefore propose to express my thanks to them all for their assistance in certain broad categories.

It goes without saying that I owe an enormous debt to the British Museum and to the Bibliothèque Nationale, and especially to Mr. H. M. Nixon and to M. Guignard respectively.

Secondly, I must thank the many learned French municipal librarians for all the help which they have given me, whether by their own researches into their archives, by consulting local almanachs, etc., or by enlisting the co-operation of local connoisseurs. If I have badgered any of them on occasion to the point where they furnished me with information almost out of desperation, I trust that they will excuse my importunity in a worthy cause.

And then, I owe a deep debt of gratitude to the second-hand booksellers of France and the U.K., and indeed of many other countries, for their patient aid to an amateur, who perhaps did not always buy what they would have liked to have sold him, but wanted something just a little different, or more difficult. Their solid corps of knowledge has been invaluable to me.

And lastly, thanks to the many who have written to me out of the blue, or who have responded to a barely audible signal, from within this country, from France, Belgium, Holland, the U.S.A., and even from the Antipodes; in fact from all over the world.

I hope that this book will not prove a disappointment to all or any of the above, that they will accept my heartfelt thanks for their past help, and that they will let me know anything of interest which may supplement what I have been able to collect to date.

CHARLES RAMSDEN,
171, Queen's Gate,
London, S.W.7.

INTRODUCTION

The object of this work is not to present a complete or a technical picture of French bookbinding between two dates convenient from a political or a cultural point of view. It is a more modest one, that of gathering together as many facts as possible regarding those craftsmen who contributed substantially to French bookbinding during the period under review (1789–1848).

In preparing a work of this kind for publication, it is perhaps desirable for one who has no obvious capability for undertaking such a task, to explain as briefly as possible his reasons for so doing. My main reason is that my studies on this subject have been a labour of love which has often offered me complete escape or refreshment from less congenial tasks.

Towards the end of the Second World War I first became really interested in French bindings of what can be roughly called the Romantic Period, I soon found that no adequate and collected documentation on the subject was available in a published form.

Thoinan's excellent work, as well as those of Gruel and Marius Michel (I am not referring to Marius Michel's work dated 1881 on industrial and commercial binding), stop at about the end of the eighteenth century. The main work which attempts to deal with the following period, namely, Béraldi's "La Reliure au XIXe Siècle" Volumes I and II, besides being printed in a very limited edition of 295 copies and very difficult to procure, is now over fifty years out of date. Its author, despite —and perhaps because of—his wide range of interests, was not very sympathetic to even the best products of a period too near to him to be judged in its proper perspective. The sale catalogue of Béraldi's own collection, compiled about fifteen years ago, only lists seventy binders (some of whom he exhibits with pride as almost unknown) as against the approximate 1500 binders listed in this work, which makes no claim to be exhaustive.

The collector of almost any author of even moderate repute from the beginning of the sixteenth century onwards finds little difficulty in laying his hands on such bibliographical details of the works of his favourite as to enable him to form a very fair idea of what he has to look for in order to form a representative collection.

On the other hand, I was constantly noticing, partly from sale catalogues and far more from personal observation, numerous binders of the period who appeared to possess merit, but at the same time to be virtually unknown even to collectors or booksellers otherwise interested in the literature of the period. I gradually came to the conclusion that, though the information which I had gathered was somewhat haphazard, it represented something worthy of record. I therefore set to work to systematise my notes, and this led to my finding myself faced with the question of the degree of selectivity, if any, which I should exercise in recording the binders of the epoch.

My first feelings were in favour of excluding any binders of whose excellency I was not personally satisfied. From that point of view I have since radically departed, for the reasons set forth below:

(i) The list of binders with which I started, barely exceeding 200, has swollen rapidly to about 1500.

(ii) This increase has been due (a) to my own researches among the Parisian and provincial almanachs, and (b) to most valuable assistance from many French provincial librarians, bringing to light much of the greatest novelty and interest.

(iii) The gradual emergence of quite a number of bookbinders possibly known to me or to one or two other people, but as to whose artistic standing, or even as to particulars of where or when they worked, nothing had been recorded.

(iv) Arising from (iii), a doubt occurred in my own mind as to whether I was justified in deciding not to put on record information gathered or provided with difficulty, and which may in the future provide clues which are badly needed. The binder virtually unknown to-day may well be later the esteemed artist regarding whom any scrap of information is of value, and increasingly difficult to discover.

With the above considerations in mind, I have listed in the index, which forms the main body of this work, all those who I am reasonably sure "bound" during the period 1789–1848. I have included the more eminent ancillary workers of the bookbinding fraternity, such as gilders, marblers, stitchers, gatherers, restorers, etc., but have, perhaps rather arbitrarily, excluded sellers of varnish, and other furnishings.

In connection with those whom I have listed, I have given, wherever available, particulars as to: (i) their Christian names, parentage, etc.; (ii) the dates of their births and deaths; (iii) their addresses; (iv) the years during which they were active; (v) details of their apprenticeships, partnerships, etc.; (vi) references to sources of information, and, on occasion, brief personal appreciations. (As to illustrations, see below.)

I should like to have reproduced a few portraits of eminent binders of the period; it is, however, a strange fact that at most only one portrait of any known binder of the epoch seems to have survived, or at least to have been noted. Then, no doubt, it was not thought worth while; now the gap cannot be filled.

Illustrations

A work of this kind would, in my opinion, lose much of its value if it contained no illustrations of bindings of the period. Apart from the question of the cost of reproducing many plates, it is obviously undesirable to give a merely picture-book attraction to a serious work by inserting a given number of reproductions of the books of such artists as the Bozérians, Chaumont, Courteval, Doll, Simier, Thouvenin, Purgold, etc., which are readily available elsewhere. My object has, therefore, been to enable my readers to study the work of the lesser-known binders, or the lesser-known aspects of the more famous (a) by indicating where such bindings are illustrated and/or described in works which are fairly readily accessible (see Bibliography), and (b) by supplementing such indications with illustrations of similar work from my own collection or other sources, so as to provide a "corpus" which may be of real use.

French Binders Working Outside France

One of the questions which I have had to face is whether, and to what extent, I should include in my index French binders working outside France, such as the Comte de Caumont, and even foreign binders such as Lodigiani (Milan), working so closely on French lines as to be virtually indistinguishable from French binders except on grounds of domicile. I have dealt with this difficulty in a way which I do not claim to be logical, but which I hope my readers may find to be culturally justified. In adopting such a somewhat loose classification, I have been influenced by the important role played by German and English binders in French binding of the time.

Belgian Binders

I must confess that this aspect of the immediately preceding question has caused me considerable doubts. The close literary, artistic, and even political ties between France and Belgium have necessarily implied intercourse from the binding point of view, and it has even been difficult on occasions to know if a given binder should be classed as French or Belgian. For some years I adopted the system of noting Belgian binders when they came my way, with any available particulars, but not going out of my way to hunt them out, e.g., by interrogating the Brussels and provincial libraries.

Quite recently, however, I have learnt that a distinguished binder, living in Belgium, is in process of preparing a history of Belgian binding. I have therefore found myself in the happy position of giving him my notes on Belgian binders 1789–1848, and receiving from him (to my eternal gratitude) far more copious notes on French binders which he had collected. So this aspect of my problem has been solved, though I shall keep my specimens of Schavye, Deflinne, etc., on my shelves.

Unsigned Bindings

There is no more fascinating, nor deceptive game than trying to identify an unsigned binding as the work of a known binder. I have played it hard myself and enjoyed every moment of it, but I would urge my readers to regard it as an amusement and not as a science. There are cases where it comes off, such as the seated Indian goddess on a stamped velvet, figured in Béraldi's Reliure, plate 58, knowing which I bought a similar "unsigned" binding, and found the signature upside down on the back cover. But I have chanced my arm, in the catalogue of an important exhibition, on a cathedral binding which I ventured to ascribe publicly to Thouvenin, or Vogel, on the basis of a "chrysanthemum" border, which I have since seen on the work of other binders.

I am now more interested in tracing the persistence of tools through a series of binders. It is obvious that, in general, the makers of binders' tools made a range which were available to all comers, though a reference to Thouvenin Jeune in the index will show that he was most careful in ordering his *own* tools. There is much further research work to be done on this subject, both on such aspects as the exactly similar motifs employed by Simier and Schavye on their mosaic bindings; the shell tool which I have seen on bindings by Thouvenin, Chilliat, and Serre; the goffer plate used by Capé and Libermann (q.v.); the tools employed almost simultaneously by Gaudreau and de Beauvais (q.v.), etc., etc. The fact that the present whereabouts of Thouvenin's specimen book (Gum. xii. No. 351) is unknown is a matter for real regret.

Domicile from the Historical Point of View

Anyone who examines the index of binders in this work must be struck by the fact that, despite the disappearance of the old guilds during the Revolution, binding continued to be concentrated in certain streets, such as: Sept-Voies; St. Jacques; St. Jean-de-Beauvais; Charretière; Carmes; St. Hilaire, etc., etc. It might well be worth while for a dweller in these quarters to compile an index from the point of view of (i) the binder(s) in question; (ii) the number in the individual street where he lived; (iii) the years of residence, etc. A properly prepared schedule might throw much light on problems of apprenticeship, relationship, etc.

Provincial Binders

Up to about the end of 1948, the vast majority of the binders of whom I had any records were Parisian. Since then I have made an appeal to the librarians of provincial towns in France to remedy this situation. Without citing individual towns or librarians, the results have been quite astonishing. I owe them all my heartiest thanks for their very kind response to my approaches, and I am glad through their help to be able to give a new lease of life to some very deserving artists.

Dates

As regards the binders whom I have recorded towards the end of our period, I have not in general troubled to pursue their careers after about 1848-50, but it must not be assumed that certain of them were not working long after those dates.

A SKETCH
OF FRENCH BOOKBINDING
1789–1848

It would diminish the value of the details presented in alpha-betical order regarding individual binders which form the bulk of this study, if they were not accompanied by at least a brief outline of the principal sub-divisions of the period from such points of view as changes in taste, technical proficiency, materials, etc.

The following sections of this introduction will deal with these aspects on a scale which, it is hoped, will be adequate, without being over-elaborate.

1789 – 1800

Writers on French binding have in the past tended to the opinion that the art which flourished up to the end of the year 1789 suffered an almost complete eclipse from that date and only revived about fifteen years later under the Consulate and early Empire. Such a view, though containing some elements of truth, is, however, too drastic to be accepted without reservations.

It is true that, as the Revolution grew in violence, more and more of the richer and noble classes, who had been notable patrons of the arts, including those affecting fine book production, either fled abroad, or suffered eclipse at home. Many fine libraries were destroyed, and to their eternal shame some bookbinders offered their services to remove the armorial decorations from the bind-ings of the "ancienne noblesse". In such circumstances few orders for fine bindings could be expected; in fact life was far too hazardous for such luxuries.

Probably, therefore, it can be said that there was little or no fine binding done between 1793–98, though some notable binders survived over these years, either living on their resources or finding other temporary work. Some of the Bradel family seem to have been active right from before 1789 to well on in the 1820s. Tessier, who started as binder to the Comte d'Artois before the Revolution and changed his labels and appointments with notable facility several times up to 1815, became, after the Restoration, binder to the Duc d'Orleans. Simier first started to bind about 1798, after leaving the army. In 1801 J. C. Bozérian, in publishing and editing J. J. Rousseau in twenty-five volumes printed by Didot (Gum. xii, 332), was already describing himself as "relieur".

A correct summary of the position from 1793 to the first years of the nineteenth century would probably be that taste in bookbinding was dormant, that patrons, other than institutional, were rare and hard up, and that materials were poor in quality. Such was the lack of orders that Lesné, though trained as a bookbinder, only started to practise in 1802, having meanwhile worked as a carpenter.

1800 – 1815

Before attempting to define the main divisions into which the bindings of this period can be classified, it may be wise to make a few general reservations:

(i) While it is generally true that binding in France did not reach full expression again until the creation of the Empire, the beginnings of the revival were apparent, if not obvious, during the Consulate and can probably be traced back to the Directorate.

(ii) It is easy, but probably misleading, to attach too much artistic importance to the work of the two Bozérian brothers during the period under consideration. They were both capable on occasion of really good work executed to special order, even if it is seldom of the highest artistic order. The vast majority of Bozérian bindings nowadays offered to the public consists of the output of their well organised and efficient bulk binderies. These generally produced excellent work from the technical point of view, which looks well on bookshelves in large quantities, but has little artistic value and has no feel "in the hand".

(iii) The constant state of hostilities in which France found herself during the period, the uncertainty of her overseas relations, and the upstart nature of most of her ruling classes were responsible for such common, though by no means general, defects in binding as inferior design, and the poor quality of the leather, gold, and other materials employed.

Subject to the above remarks, the bindings of the period 1800–15 can be sub-divided as follows:

(a) Utility binding. This seems to have been done in the main, and very competently, by the Bozérian brothers: at any rate no other binders of the period seem to have lent their signature to such bulk binding. The Bozérians had a limited range of patterns and colours for this class of work and (*pace* Lesné-Dibden) it represented little difference from, or advance on, similar work already being done in England.

(b) At the other end of the scale there was a growing demand for work of a high-class and even an ostentatious character. This tended at first to be on traditional eighteenth-century lines, such as those followed by Bradel from before 1789 right on into the Restoration. Towards 1804, however, this class of binding divides into two rather separate lines, which may be classified as "semi-luxury", dealt with under (d) below, and "swagger" bindings.

(c) The "swagger" bindings, which personify the triumphs of France from 1797–1812, have many features which recall the wide range of countries and civilisations with which France was brought into contact during those years, as well as the Greek and Latin spirit which has always been close to French thought and was especially congenial to Napoleon. It is now fashionable to decry the formal spirals and scrolls, the harps and classical and mythological figures, the emblems and animals which decorate many fine bindings of the period, but it is hard to deny that they

3

are first-class work. They represent the translation into the art of bookbinding of a phase of art which not only had its epochal importance, but added something to the sum of the world's artistic history. The use of classical symbols and devices was largely developed by bookbinders (some of them provincial) such as: Lefébvre, Mairet (Dijon), Courteval, Lodigiani (Milan), Tessier, etc., etc., and was equally employed by English binders of about the same period (though their use in England may have started a little earlier than in France).

(d) Perhaps the most interesting aspect of French bookbinding of this period, for the ordinary collector, is that of the orders by the person who wanted a first-class binding on the book which had taken his fancy without launching out into the luxury class. He had a very wide choice of binders: not only the Bozérians and the Bradels who dominated the market, but also such artists as Doll, Chilliat, Courteval, Lefébvre, Meslant, etc., and better still, the future "grand-maitres"—Thouvenin, Simier, and Purgold are all well in the field by 1805. It is true that they had their bad feature in their sloppy backs, almost hidden in "pointillé" gold, which produced an ugly "slurred" effect, but they were nevertheless developing tools which would serve them greatly in the succeeding period.

1815 — 1830

It was probably not before 1819 that the style of binding known first as "Restoration" and later as "Romantic" definitely emerged, though the movement may have started very soon after 1815. A binding in my possession by Bozérian Jeune, who is believed to have retired from business in 1818, bears a typical Romantic blindstamp which, in view of the state and unimportance of the binding in question, seems unlikely to have been added at a later date.

The general characteristics of the bindings of the period are constant, despite the great variety and inventiveness of their external decoration. They are: (i) excellent workmanship; (ii) both

4

apparent and real solidity; (iii) flat as opposed to rounded backs; (iv) spine bands, if apparent at all, are more often false than a result of the stitching of the binder; (v) the gold employed for ornamentation is of excellent quality; (vi) titles on the spine are generally given in full, in opposition to the often ridiculous abbreviations employed in the eighteenth and preceding centuries; (vii) the general exterior decoration is as efficient and well executed as the main run of later eighteenth-century work was slovenly; (viii) the quality of the leather, especially the morocco, is excellent and its colour range, as compared with Bozérian's four-colour scheme, is practically unlimited. Much of the leather is now of French manufacture. The colour range of calf was also greatly amplified, though the somewhat meretricious marbled effects popular in the 1800–15 period tended to disappear.

Another particularly pleasing feature of the period is the wide use of half bindings. Their execution is usually of the same high order as that of the full bindings, but the necessary concentration of all decoration on the spine is often a positive advantage, as the binder (and under his guidance the toolcutter) often produced effects of great brilliance and charm.

The Triumviri

The 1815–30 period is dominated by three great figures, Simier, Purgold, and Thouvenin. The first-named started binding about 1798, and all three were executing competent bindings in the style of the First Empire by about 1805. All three were able to adapt themselves to the taste of the Restoration and continued to dominate their field until about 1830. They all display the highest order of workmanship in their bindings.

An attempt to judge the relative merits of each of the three as a binder is an invidious but an unavoidable task.

Simier is perhaps the most adaptable of the three; there appears to be no style, old or new, of which he could not make himself an easy and a competent master. While he could on occasion produce a supreme masterpiece of elegance and simplicity, his work for his royal and princely patrons too often led him into excesses of decoration and gilding in which all sense of design tended to disappear. Of the three great binders of the period, Simier is, to my mind, the one of whom it is easiest to have a surfeit. From the point of view of productivity, he and Thouvenin run each other very close.

Purgold is perhaps the best binder of the three from a technical point of view, but also seems, without any conscious attempt at imitation, to have absorbed the pre-eighteenth-century spirit of European binding. His productions, though often having a tendency to heaviness in design, have a richness which is not dependent on over-gilding. He could on occasion be a master of the straight line, an art which he passed on to Bauzonnet. Within the limitations of his range (and it is limited) he is perhaps the greatest of the three. He is also in spirit, as in name, the least French of the three.

Thouvenin is the most interesting. While he had the wide range of Simier, he had a spirit of invention, which neither of the other two possessed, combined with high technical ability. Perhaps his greatest achievement is to be found in the very chaste and sober bindings, usually in dark blue morocco, made for Charles Nodier, bearing on one side "Ex Musaeo Caroli Nodier" and on the other "Ex officina Jos. Thouvenin". Unfortunately, however, Nodier in Thouvenin's last years encouraged him to an imitation of old French bindings which his talent made an easy task for him, but which was to end in the eclipse of the brilliant period of original binding in which Thouvenin had been perhaps the brightest star.

The predominance of these three great binders does not, however, mean that individuality was confined to them alone. In fact, one of the fascinations of the period is the wide range of more modest but still important or charming binders, and it is easy for anyone with a little experience to recognise the work of Ginain, Carroll, Meslant, Ducastin, Vogel, and many others from some personal note.

In the preceding period and in the first years after the Restoration most of the external decoration of bindings appears to have been hand-applied by the use of fine tools, rollers, etc., but it was not long before heavier tools, possibly imported from England, were in common use. Slightly later we notice whole centre or corner plaques being used to produce by pressure large ornaments either in gilt or in blind. Finally, plaques were prepared which could be used, direct or in reverse, on both sides of a binding simultaneously to cover its whole surface. This process was usually executed in blind, additional gilt ornamentation constituting a separate operation. The whole process constitutes a return to the method employed four to five hundred years ago to calf or vellum monastic bindings. It was applied first with great skill to bindings destined for the more exacting class of client, and only later and less skillfully to prize books, etc.

Consideration of such stamped bindings leads inevitably to the so-called "Cathedral" or Neo-Gothic bindings, which do not, however, constitute an isolated phenomenon. They are only a part of a belated, and not too "informed" rediscovery of Gothic art, which in our own country influenced taste from the time of Beckford's Fonthill Abbey to the Eglinton Tournament. Neo-Gothic influence spread to many aspects of public and domestic life, architecture, dress, decoration, poetry, etc., and binding was bound to be affected. Its influence on exterior book decoration was perhaps greater and more inappropriate than in most other directions. Large formalised cathedral fronts applied haphazard to the bindings of completely incongruous works are hardly bearable. Only when such plaques show a certain naïveté, or are limited to isolated "Gothic" features have they a "period" charm. Even so they should be in blind, with little or no gilt.

"Neo-Gothic" leads on to "Mosaic". Occasional examples of this form of decoration had lingered on from the age of Grolier, through the eighteenth-century Court bindings to the days of the

Empire. There is little doubt that a study of Gothic architecture, and especially of its stained glass, led to a desire to add the attraction of elaborate colour effects to the existing "cathedral" style of binding. This was accomplished by complicated "appliqués" of coloured leather, coupled with a heightening of gilt effects. The results, apart from the technical efficiency of the performance, were generally disastrous. Except where the range of colours was kept down to two or three at most, a sixpenny kaleidoscope would have been preferable and better value.

1830–48

This period, though it has many brilliant features, must from the bookbinding point of view be regarded as one of decadence. One great binder, Bauzonnet, came into a prominence which he maintained till his death about the end of the period. He was able, usually by quite simple methods and especially by reliance on straight lines, to produce effects which on occasion show supreme elegance.

Two notable classes of binders emerged: (i) an overflow from the previous period still doing excellent work such as: Muller (successor of Thouvenin), Koehler, Duplanil, Blaise, A. Simier, Germain-Simier, Ducastin, Comélaran, Debès, Ginain, Thouvenin Jeune, Crabbe, Bonfils, etc., etc.; (ii) a number of newcomers such as: Trautz, Capé, Duru, Petit, Thompson, Niedrée, Hardy, etc., whose early work, approximating to that of the previous period, is often good, but whose later productions tend to lose all individual initiative, and, far worse, to serve as an excuse for a vandalism of rebinding which is one of the worst features of mid-nineteenth-century "taste".

The following general features are worthy of note:
(a) technical execution remains at a high level;
(b) the morocco employed tends to change from the straight-grain of the previous period, with its exquisite feel, to a rather close-grained shagreen or sealskin effect, which is far less pleasing to the eye and touch;

8

(c) the gold employed, except for the more luxury bindings, seems to be less solid, and less resistant to wear and tear;

(d) rounded backs succeed the flat backs of the previous period, while raised bands on the spine become the exception rather than the rule. This change, in the author's modest opinion, still continues a hundred years later to exercise an evil influence, for however excellent the sides of modern French bindings may be, their backs are rounded and "spineless".

As regards the broader aspects of external decoration, the main tendencies, as the period advances and especially from 1840 to 1850, are: (1) towards exaggerated copying or adaptation of the French bindings of the fifteenth to seventeenth centuries and (2) towards a bastard form of eighteenth-century binding, with plain-centred sides, surrounded by over-elaborate patterns of rather finicky tooling in gilt and backs submerged in gilt filigrane. Such bindings have little or no originality, while, quâ copies, they are as like their originals as a "Viollet-le-Duc" Carcassonne, or Pierrefonds.

About 1838–40 "to order" binding suffered a severe blow from the establishment of "industrial" binderies by Engel and Lenègre. These binderies not only had to bind rapidly and cheaply, but, to be in a position to do so, had to have a large and constant clientèle. That meant marketing cheaply and in large quantities something striking, highly-coloured and expensive-*looking*. Hence the engraved plates by Haarhaus, Souze, and Lenègre, reproducing on the bindings illustrations from the books which they covered or "cased". Most of the illustrated "livres à succès" of the period are commonly found in the highly gilt and highly coloured publishers' bindings decorated by the use of these stereotyped plates.

The appreciation extended ten or twenty years ago to this class of industrial bindings has to-day greatly diminished, but still attaches (with some greater degree of justification) to the morocco, as opposed to the cloth specimens. It is, however, permissible to doubt whether even the "morocco" copies are any more individual bindings than their "cloth" brothers. My own feeling is that such bindings "à répétition" have little artistic and no individual value.

Almost of the same date as these publishers' bindings, and sometimes even forming part thereof, are the so-called "Louise-Philippe rocaille (rockery)" bindings. They are decorated with elaborate, blind or gilt, scrollwork, often forming a "mirror" effect on the back and sides. Boutigny was the most fertile producer of such effects, but they were also practised by the younger Simier and many others. It is seldom, however, that such productions are other than heavy and rather mechanical.

It would be easy but superfluous, I believe, to note the emergence of certain other tendencies in bookbinding between 1840 and 1848, which, however, represent fundamental deviations from, rather than developments of the 1789–1848 period as a whole. Moreover the full development of such tendencies lies rather after than before 1848, and would lead us too far afield.

BIBLIOGRAPHICAL REFERENCES, ETC.

1. A. M-S.—Alphonse Maze-Sencier: Le Livre des Collectionneurs: Librairie Renouard, 6 rue de Tournon, Paris, 1885.

2. BARTHOU.—Sale Catalogue—Louis Barthou, 5 vol. Paris, 1935–36.

2A. B. DE. F.—Bordes de Fortage: Catalogue de la Bibliothèque, 3 vol. Bordeaux, 1924.

3. BER.—H. Béraldi: Catalogue de la Bibliothèque, 5 parts, 1934–35.

4. BER. REL.—H. Béraldi: La Reliure au XIXe. 4 vol. 1895–97.

5. BOERNER, XXI.—Sale Catalogue C. G. Boerner, Leipzig, 1916.

6. DESC.—Descamps-Scrive: Bibliothèque, 3 parts, 1925. Refs., unless otherwise stated, are to Part II, Romantiques.

7. D. D'E.—M. Dubois d'Enghien, Relieur, Heer-sur-Meuse, Belgium.

8. E. D.—Etienne Derville: Reliure Française, 2 vol. Editions van Oest, 1930–31.

9. GUM.—Gumuchian: Cat. XII, Belles Reliures, n.d.

10. LESNE.—Lesné, La Reliure, 1827.

11. MAGGS 661.—Maggs Bros. Ltd.: Catalogue de très Beaux Livres, No. 661/1938.

12. O. C.—Private Collection of C. Ramsden.

13. OLIVIER.—Manuel de l'Amateur des Reliures Armoriées Françaises, 1924–38.

14. RAHIR.—Sale Catalogue, Edouard Rahir, 6 vol., Paris, 1930–38.

15. R. L. B.—Robert L. Bach, 408, East 147th Street, New York 55.

16. ROMB.—Rombaldi: Guide du Bibliophile, an. cit.

17. SCH.—French Signed Bindings in the Schiff Collection, by S. de Ricci, 4 vol., N.Y., 1935.

18. THOINAN.—Thoinan, Les Relieurs Français (1500–1800), 1893. Thoinan is careful to mention wherever possible the exact date at which binders were "received" by the Guild as "master-binders". I myself only mention "received" and the year, as the guilds disappeared with the Revolution.

19. TROIS TETES.—Catalogue: Giraud Badin-Cornuau-Rousseau, 1936.

20. W. H.—Sale Catalogue of Mrs. G. Whitney Hoff, 2 vol., Paris, 1933.

FRENCH BINDERS OF THE 1789–1848 PERIOD, WORKING OUTSIDE PARIS, LISTED UNDER THE TOWNS WHERE THEY WERE ACTIVE

ABBEVILLE

Blondin: Dumont-Grare: Gavois-Grare: Godard: Grare.

AGEN

Dugay: Gendre: Noubel.

AIX-EN-PROVENCE

Allavène (2): Closon: Gibert.

AMIENS

Boubier: Darras: Deliège (2): Guide-Doutart: Leidler: Leprince: Serre.

ANGERS

Chartier: Chentrier: Colonier: Defody: Denis: Dubois-Canon: Duchemin: Fontaine: Gastineau: Georges: Girard: Jubeau: Maussion: Morigne: Nail: Pollane.

ANGOULEME

Wedding.

BAR-LE-DUC

Maillard.

BAYONNE

Bernain: Cluzeau: Grizy: Lecler: Lespès: Perrié: Tribouilh.

BERGERAC

Bargeas.

BESANCON

Abich: Noel.

BORDEAUX

Arnaude: Berthoud: Bichebois: Bourreau: Castera: Castillon: Cerf et Naxara: Chabrilla: Chamaison: Chataignier: Chretien: Clamouze: Delcour: Denan fils: Dorinal: Dubernet: Durre (2): Gretteau: Haring: Herbert: Hunder: Jeaussem: Jeniveau: Larrivière: Larroux: Latouche: Lavignac: Marandet: Marchand: Marfan: Massé: Melon: Mercam: Mitraud: Moinard: Monsacré: Mortier: Paget: Ponthier: Pujos: Royer: Royer et Despierres: St. Hubéri: Soudanas: Texier: Teycheney: Vinsac.

BRIENNE

Hamfin.

CAHORS

Sarazin.

CAMBRAI

Dufay: Hurez.

CLERMONT

Joyal.

DIJON

Belmet: Bulliard: Devaux: Durand: Guerrinot: Jacotier: Laroche: Mairet: Maitre: Pottié: Pradon: Verreaux.

DOLE

Dollot.

DOUAI

Fouquart (2): Ricard.

DOULLENS

Quincampoix.

DUNKIRK

Archange: Delannoy: Delettans: Paulmier.

LE MANS

Bertelage: Huet (2): Lebatteux: Lemoine.

LILLE

Arnold: Bauchet (3): Bernard: Boutoille-Petitot: Campion: Cauvin: Choquet: Couttenier: Cuignet: Dehaens (5): Delabre: Delecroix: Delfortry & Cuisinier: Delsart (2): Deruelles: Dion: Dormael: Drapier: Druart: Dufey (2): Duquesne: Gillon: Heingle: Joly: Larrivière: Leclercq: Lenfant: Libert-Petitot: Mangez: Marouf: Marouffe: Martin-Delahaye: Petitot: Platiaux: Porise: Postiau-Dufey: Renaux: Reuiller: Rousselle: Serleys: Six: Vanackère (2): Vannehin: Wignan.

LIMOGES

Audoucet: Baralet: Bardinet: Bigaud: Billonaud (2): Blémond: Bordas: Chabrol: Charles: Constant: Damet: Defay: Delomenie: Dutreuil: Estevye: Fournier (2): Germain (2): Isecq: Lagorce: Leblanc: Leblois: Malinvaud: Martin: Martinaud (2): Mathieu (2): Mesure: Meynieux: Nouhaud: Parvy: Raymond: Robert: Roby: Roche (2): Rougier: Soudanas (4): Tallnaud: Thomas: Valade: Vergne: Vinot.

LYONS

André: Artaud: Baboulat: Bailly (3): Barbier: Barre: Berioux: Bernon: Beugnet: Boeglin: Bouvet: Bruyère: Carret (3): Chavant: Dauphin: Devers (7): Dorin: Drian: Dupin (3): Dupont: Duval: Enguehard: Farge: Fassiot: Fayolle (2): Gandy: Goboz: Halmburger (4): Jager (2): Larchier (3): Laurin: Lenoir (3): Levrat: Lorin: Monniot: Nicolas: Pampin: Paquet: Penat: Petit-Guyot: Premier: Prudhomme: Sommier: Supié: Tenon: Toubillon (2): Troilon: Verziers: Vuiton.

MARSEILLES

André: Archange: Arquier: Bertrand: Blanc: Bosqui: Bouvet: Brémond: Cavalier: Choppart: Cordier: Dutertre: Foucou: Georges: Gorjux: Lagarde: Levasseur (3): Mabilly: Mathieu: Maunier: Michel: Moureau: Pic(h)on: Rey: Thobol: Touache: Trotebas: Valence: Varesy: Vellio.

METZ

Adam: Barbier: Codbat: Damel: Dargens: Dherclonville (2): Deny: Grosclaude (2): Jacob: Lanternier: Lemoine: Milard (2): Pellerin (2): Rousselot: Thiriet.

MONTDIDIER

Beauvais: Leroux: Lesueur.

MOUSSAC

Orliac.

NANCY

Dufey: Viener.

NANTES

Aubin: Belin: Bodet: Bogillot: Busseuil: Chatelier: Clebert: Cornu: Dutertre: Duval: Furret: Gallard: Gouin: Gourdaine: Gréland: Jeanneau: Jugnet: Lacoste: Lebastard: Legros: Lehoux: Lèpre: Leroux: Malati: Mazeau: Mellinet-Malassis: Plessier: Potin: Rabier: Ravard: Robertjau: Sicard: Simon: Sollier: Vétil-Sicard: Villeneuve.

ORLEANS

Auger (2): Clement: Colas (3): Cransard: Delorme: Herluison: Le Gros: Levacher: Ligot: Maurice: Paillet: Petail: Pochet (2): Quau (2): Vares.

PERONNE

Jouillard: Laisney: Trepan.

RHEIMS

Faille.

SABLE

Piron.

SAINT-OMER

Pastre.

SAINT-QUENTIN

Hautoy.

STRASSBURG

Albert: Arbogast:Auerbach: Bader: Baldner: Barmes: Bilger: Braun: Brod: Corn: Dranner: Dreyspring: Engel: Ensfelder: Fischbach: Frey: Geisler: Gezek: Girardet: Grieshaber: Guttermann: Hancké: Hartmann: Held: Hering: Hoeffel: Hoesch: Hurst: Issler: Jundt: Kamm: Kettner: Knecht (2): Koenig: Korn: Krauss: Kummerlin: Lachapelle: Lampes: Leroux: Maillot: Mathis (3): Merdel: Meyer: Müssel (2): Pfluger: Piton (2): Rayger: Redslob (2): Rhein: Riehl: Roos (2): Samuel: Schaeffer: Schenckel (2): Sommervogel: Speckel: Speich: Stamm: Stuber: Thraner: Trensz.

TOULOUSE

Abadie (3): Angelle-Bellegarde: Ayral: Bellegarde: Berny: Conte (2): Couot: Cuisinier: Darroux: Delpon: Dubois: Duperron: Garrigues: Goudoffre: Grabie: Lartet: Lartigue: Latour (2): Lichaque: Marfeillan: Marnac: Marty: Mazars: Prunet (2): Revel: Rey: Sage (3): Senac: Simonet: Soulas: Vabre (3): Vincens.

TOURS

Cocheu: Mame.

VERSAILLES

Langlois

17

ALPHABETICAL INDEX OF BINDERS

ABADIE   *Toulouse*

Noted in 1807 "près de la place Perchepinte".

ABADIE, Père   *Toulouse*

Worked in 1838 at rue de la Fonderie.

ABADIE, Auguste   *Toulouse and Paris*

Probably the same as Abadie Fils, who worked at St. Etienne 22, Toulouse, in 1838. Thoinan possessed a copy of Abadie's poems dated 1853, and bound by the author possibly at the same date. A French bookseller's catalogue dated January 1949 mentions a copy of Grandville's *Fleurs Animées*, undated, bound by him.

The volume of Abadie's poems cited by Thoinan in a postscript on p. 340 is described as *Roses et Dahlias*, Toulouse '53, in – 12°, limited to 20 copies. The volume in question mentions another edition in – 8°. Thoinan states that Abadie eventually left Toulouse for Paris, where he had a second-hand book shop on the Quai Voltaire, and where he died about 1864.

ABBA

Signature reported by D. d'E. on a work dated 1820.

ABELARD

Probably worked between 1835–40. A binding by him is mentioned in the B. de F. Cat. No. 32.

ABICH   *Besançon*

He was probably active about 1840, as Maggs' Cat. 661/243 refers to a contemporary binding by him on the Bourdin 1001 *Nuits* (n.d., but known to have been published in 1840). He affected a neat rocaille style, often on citron morocco. He styles himself "Relieur Gainier, rue St. Paul 43 à Besançon" on a half-calf binding in my own collection.

ABRAHAM   *Paris*

Mentioned in the 1847–49 Almanachs as at Parcheminerie 2.

ABRY   *Colmar*

Worked at rue du Fromage 9 about 1802. For an elaborate ecclesiastical binding which might well date 15 to 20 years earlier, see Sch. II. 207.

ADAM   *Paris*

A binder of this name worked in 1827 at rue Bleue 27, when he received an honourable mention at the Paris Exhibition for his "mobile" bindings. A binding signed Adam in a rocaille style in my own collection appears to date much nearer 1844.

ADAM, Joseph (and bookseller)   *Metz*

Apprenticed in 1774 and set up in 1782 at rue de la Tête d'Or. Died December 2, 1824.

AGASSE, Satiner   *Paris*

Appears in the 1815 Almanach at Sept Voies 11.

ALBERT, Jean-Wolfgang   *Strassburg*

Working at Place de la Grande Boucherie 33 in 1824.

ALLAVENE, Père   *Aix*

The 1822 Almanach mentions him at rue du Collège.

ALLAVENE, Fils   *Aix*

Noted at rue des Grands Carmes in 1822.

AMAND

Nothing is known to me of him, beyond his name.

ANDRE, Claude-Gaspard   *Lyons*

Appears at rue Ferranderie 25 in 1810, and at No. 13 from 1813–16.

ANDRE *Marseilles*

Started at rue 1ᵉʳ Calade 4 in 1847 and moved next year to rue des Fabres 43.

ANDREAU

Only his name is known to me.

ANDRIEU *Paris*

I have him noted as a binder of the period (*c.* 1838). For confirmation see Dupré.

ANDRIEUX *Paris*

Active probably from 1837 to as late as 1863. He figures at Ste. Anne 11 in the Almanachs 1840–49, first as binder to the Orleans princes and to the University of Paris, and after 1848 to the National Assembly. For illustrations of his work see Maggs' Cat. 661/255 and Desc. 234.

ANGELLE-BELLEGARDE *Toulouse*

Worked at rue d'Astorg 46 in 1847.

ARBOGAST, Th. *Strassburg*

At Grand'rue 148 in 1846.

ARCHANGE *Dunkirk*

Appears in the 1788 Almanach for Dunkirk at rue des Prêtres.

ARCHANGE *Marseilles*

Worked between 1819–48 in the rue d'Aubagne 63 ('19): 60 ('25), and 66 ('41).

ARNAUD *Paris*

The 1847–49 Almanachs give him as working at Monsieur-le-Prince 11.

ARNAUDE *Bordeaux*

At rue du Temple 6 in 1848.

ARNAUX   *Paris*

Worked at Judas 13 in 1838 and at Clos Bruneau 13 in 1840–42.

ARNOLD, André   *Lille*

Active between 1824–48. A binding by him is mentioned in Desc. II, No. 47. See also Rombaldi 47/A 690. His addresses were: rue Royale 41; rue de la Barre 25 ('36).

ARNOWSKI   *Paris*

Known from the Almanachs to have worked between 1843–49. His first address was Serpente 3, and later ('47) Parcheminerie 2.

ARQUIER   *Marseilles*

Worked between 1841–44 at rue Maucouinat 25.

ARTAUD   *Lyons*

His particular signature hidden among the scrollwork at the base of the spine is mentioned in Gruel ('05), II, p. 20, but he may fall outside our period.

AUBERT   *Paris*

An unidentified member of the family is given in the Almanach Typographique of 1799 as at rue Louis, au ci-devant Marais.

AUBERT, Jean-Baptiste   *Paris*

Worked in Paris, first at rue des Carmes, and then at rue Charretière, between 1766–90. He is mentioned by Thoinan on pp. 192 and 271, and was one of the sons-in-law of J. B. Duplanil I.

AUBERT, Jean-Louis   *Paris*

According to Thoinan, p. 192, he was received as a master-binder in 1733, and lived at rue Charretière till 1776. He was still alive in 1790, but can hardly have been practising.

AUBERT, Joseph   *Paris*

Received as master-binder in 1759, and lived at rue Charretière till 1790.

AUBIN   *Nantes*

Worked "vis-à-vis de St. Similien" between 1841–44.

AUDIGER   *Chartres*

Bookseller and binder in 1839.

AUDOUCET   *Limoges*

Master-binder 1756–89.

AUERBACH, Baer   *Strassburg*

Noted in 1824 at Coin Brûle 4.

AUGER   *Orleans*

At rue Faverie in 1846.

AUGER   *Paris*

Mentioned by Thoinan, p. 193, as already working in 1800. His
address in 1803 was St. Jacques 627 and in 1809 No. 124 of the same
street.

AUGER-JACOB   *Orleans*

Worked in 1832 at rue des Petits-Souliers.

AURI   *Paris*

The 1832–38 Almanachs give his address as Foin St. Jacques 9. It is
possible that in 1832 he may have been at No. 7.

AVISSE   *Paris*

Figures in the Almanachs between 1821–49 at the following addresses: Foin St. Jacques 28 ('21); St. Jean-de-Beauvais 13 ('32);
No. 24 ('35); Lune 37 ('42).

AVONDE

This quite unknown binder's signature figures at the base of the spine
on a school-prize binding in my own collection on Mme. Bernard's
Théâtre des Marionettes, 1837.

AYRAL   *Toulouse*

"Près du Rempart" in 1780, and rue St. Rome in 1807.

BABOULAT, Jean-Baptiste   *Lyons*

Appears in 1842 at rue Petit-David.

BADER, J.   *Strassburg*

Worked at Mineure 5 in 1846.

BADIEJOUS   *Toulouse*

His name figures on a Basque Grammar, formerly the property of the Duchesse de Berry, illustrated in Quaritch 1921, Cat. No. 287, and in Desc. II, No. 64. He worked between 1807–48 as follows: rue Vinaigre ('07); Trinité ('33); Peyras 26 ('37).

BAILLIEUX   *Paris*

Figures in the 1847–49 Almanachs as binding at Neuve-Ste. Geneviève 30.

BAILLY, Joseph   *Lyons*

Worked between 1810–16 at Hospice (or Hôpital) 14.

BAILLY, Pierre   *Lyons*

This member of the family is first found in 1810 at Place Confort 8, then at No. 13 in 1813, and lastly at Raisin 5 in 1821.

BAILLY, Pierre-Philippe   *Lyons*

Worked in rue Ferranderie as follows: No. 23 ('10); 9 ('13); 14 ('15); and 9 ('21).

BAILLY   *Paris*

Specialised in edge-gildings. Addresses: St. Jean-de-Beauvais 41 ('40); 11 ('42); St. Jacques 67 ('47); 59 ('49).

BAINSE   *Paris*

First appears at Petit Reposoir 6 in 1838, and then in 1842 at St. Marc 33 and Montmartre 40.

BALDNER, M. *Strassburg*

    Working at Finckwiller 56 in 1846.

BALONCHARD *Paris*

    According to the Almanachs was active at Chartres 24 between 1847–49.

BARALET (*also Barralet and Baralhé*) *Limoges*

    At rue Fourie in 1836 and Place St. Pierre (1846–48).

BARBA, *Henri Frédéric, Fils Aîné* *Paris*

    This binder, though I have not been able to see a specimen of his work, appears to have tried to cut a considerable dash between 1837 –43. He advertised himself as having 2000 sample bindings on exhibition. His addresses were successively: St. Jacques 38 and Vivienne 1 ('37); St. Hyacinthe 8 and Vivienne 1 ('38); Sorbonne 4 ('42).

BARBA, *Veuve Prosper* *Paris*

    She was a sewer and gatherer, working at St. Jacques 59 from 1815–16. There is no trace, as far as I know, of any activity of her husband in the binding line.

BARBIER, *Claude-Auguste* *Lyons*

    Appears in the 1842 guide at Paradis 2.

BARBIER, *Joseph (and bookseller)* *Metz*

    Born at Metz, November 13, 1738. He set up on the Place d'Armes, where he lived till his death in 1811.

BARBIER, *Nicolas* *Paris*

    According to Thoinan, p. 202, he was received in 1776 and lived in rue Charretière. According to the 1803 Almanach he was still working there at No. 4.

BARDINET, *Michel* *Limoges*

    Master-binder in 1789.

BARET

According to Béraldi, Lesné mentions his addiction to the bottle.

BARGEAS *Bergerac*

An American informant says that he was active between 1777 and 1800, and cites a ticket "Relié par Bargeas, Libraire et Relieur".

BARMES, G. *Strassburg*

Appears at Quai des Bâteliers 9 in 1846.

BARRE, *Veuve* *Lyons*

Noted in the 1832 Lyons Guide at Place de la Miséricorde 7.

BARTHELEMY *Paris*

The 1842–49 Almanachs give his address as St. Jean-de-Beauvais 14.

BARTHELEMY *Paris*

At Foin-St. Jacques 10 in 1842.

BASIN *Paris*

Mentioned by Lesné as a first-class gilder.

BATAILLE *Paris*

Gruel II, p. 291, mentions him at rue des Carmes, près St. Hilaire.

BATILLOT, *Louis-Etienne* *Paris*

He received his mastership in 1749, and though he was still alive, according to Thoinan, p. 203, in 1790, it would hardly appear that he can be counted as a binder of the period with which this work deals.

BATTUT *Boulogne*

The Annuaires note him as a binder and stationer between 1844–47 at Wissocq 7.

BAUCHET *Lille*

Worked at rue du Théâtre 9 in 1844.

BAUCHET-CATEL   *Lille*

Active 1845–48.

BAUCHET-VERLINDE   *Lille*

Addresses: rue des Sept Sauts 1 ('36); Place du Théâtre 27 ('44).

BAUDET   *Paris*

Appears in the Almanachs between 1797–1821 at the following addresses: St. Victor 22 ('97); St. Jean-de-Beauvais 30 ('15).

BAUDRY, *Thomas*   *Paris*

The only mention of this binder which I have been able to trace is in the 1826 Paris Almanach at Blancs Manteaux 27.

BAUER, *Frédéric*   *Paris*

Worked between 1838–42 at Petits-Pères 7.

BAUTIER   *Paris*

Mentioned in the Almanach Typographique of 1799 and in the 1803 Almanach at Sept Voies 27.

BAUTIER   *Paris*

The Almanach Typographique 1799 gives his address as rue Bordet.

BAUZONNET, A.   *Paris*

Though not working on his own till after Purgold's death in 1830, he was one of the great binders of the period before 1848, in which year he died. In 1829 he had evidently been associated with Purgold for some years, and signed bindings as Bauzonnet-Purgold, under which name he worked for some years after succeeding Purgold and marrying his widow. He later worked under his own name, and finally as Bauzonnet-Trautz (*q.v.*). He appears in the Almanachs as follows: Cassette 18 ('32); Four-St. Germain 17 ('36). For illustrations see Bér. Rel. II, plates 48/50. I have an excellent binding dedicated by the author, E. Gros, to F. Guizot about 1835 and with the latter's initials on the sides.

BAUZONNET-PURGOLD *Paris*

There seems no doubt that Bauzonnet used this style from 1829 to a
few years after Purgold's death in 1830. In his early years of indepen-
dence he concentrated on the development of Purgold's straight line
technique (see Desc. II, 363), and achieved a supreme mastery therein,
which is reflected in many Parisian bindings about 115 years later.
Excellent reproductions of their bindings occur in Béraldi's Reliure,
Vol. II, plates 46 and 47.

BAUZONNET-TRAUTZ *Paris*

Trautz was born in 1808 and died in 1879. After being a gilder to
Kleinhans and Debès, he entered Bauzonnet's employ in 1833 and
became his partner in 1840. In the meantime he had married Mlle.
Purgold, Bauzonnet's step-daughter. In 1847 the firm was signing as
Bauzonnet et Trautz at Honoré Chevalier 10. After Bauzonnet's
death the firm was known as Trautz-Bauzonnet. A good example of
the firm's work is described and illustrated in Desc. II, 260.

BAYARD *Paris*

Though he is listed in the 1842–43 Almanachs as a binder, working
at Faubourg St.-Martin 51, he appears to have operated chiefly as a
newspaper shop.

BAZIN, *Jacques* *Paris*

Thoinan, p. 203, refers to him as active in the rue Sept Voies in 1767.
He is possibly the same as the binder quoted in the 1797–98
Almanachs as working at Faubourg St. Antoine 235.

BAZIN, *Pierre* *Paris*

His address is given by Thoinan, p. 204, as rue Ecosse in 1790. He
was a gilder, and apparently offered with a member of the Padeloup
family to remove gilt armorials from books in the Bibliothèque
Nationale.

BAZIN *Paris*

Appears in the Almanachs 1842–47 as working at Boucheries St.
Germain 15.

BEAUCHAMP *Paris*

A binder and restorer, appears in the 1826 Almanach with address at Boulevard Poissonnière 17.

BEAUVAIS, Alexᵉ. de. (also see CHAPRON) *Paris*

Probably worked between 1809–18. A ticket in my possession gives his address as rue de l'Observance 7, près l'Ecole de Médecine, which is confirmed in the 1815 Almanach. The binding in my collection on *Les Folies du Siècle* by Lourdoueix, half-morocco, paper sides, is interesting as showing on the base of the spine tools used by Gaudreau (*q.v.*) on a binding of about the same date.

BEAUVAIS *Montdidier*

Practised at rue de Roye in 1826.

BECQUET *Paris*

Shown in the 1797–98 Almanachs as working at rue des Pères 9.

BECQUET *Paris*

Figures in Almanachs from 1797–1815, first at Place Cambrai 4 and then at Cloître St. Benoit 12. Lesné ('27) on p. 340 refers to a Becquet, who may well be the same, as "unknown".

BECQUET, Fils *Paris*

Appears at Chaumière 1039 in the 1803 Almanach.

BEDOILLE

Only his name is known to me.

BELACHE *Paris*

Shown as a binder's furnisher in the 1842–47 Almanach with address at Arbre Sec 48.

BELLAIN *Nantes*

Worked 1828–44 as follows: Place Bourbon; Place du Pilory ('32); No. 12 ('43).

BELLAND   *Paris*

    Quoted by the 1842 Almanach at Passage Saucède 17.

BELLEGARDE   *Toulouse*

    First at Four-Bastard in 1780 and at Boulbonne (1807–38).

BELLIN (see BELLAIN)   *Nantes*

BELNET, Nicolas   *Dijon*

    At 48 rue Verrerie in 1836.

BENARD, Ch.

    Mentioned as responsible for a contemporary binding on Chateau-briand's Génie, 1838, in Romb. 42/3/ , A.740, and was still apparently working in 1883.

BENOIT   *Paris*

    First appears in the 1797 Almanach as working at rue des Carmes 19 and later in 1806 at rue des Amandiers. (See Thoinan, p. 205.)

BERAUD, Aîné   ? *Avignon*

    His signature appears on a half-calf binding on Nepos' *Vies des Grands Capitaines*, n.d. published at Avignon, and also on a much more elaborate morocco binding, dating about 1831, both in my own collection.

BERIOUX, Joseph   *Lyons*

    Appears in the Lyons guide at Thomassin 16 in 1810, and at No. 6 in 1813–16.

BERJOT   *Paris*

    Working between 1843 (Michodière 24) and 1849 (Neuve-Luxem-bourg 33) according to relevant Almanachs.

BERNAIN, Coralie   *Bayonne*

    Was a bookseller, stationer, and binder at Pont-Mayou 43 between 1840–50.

BERNARD   *Paris*

Appears in the 1847 Almanach as working at Racine 14.

BERNARD   *Lille*

Worked at rue des Augustins 25 in 1830.

BERNON, *Jean François*   *Lyons*

Noted in the 1821 Lyons Guide at Grande rue Mercière 54.

BERNY   *Toulouse*

At rue Bouquières in 1838.

BEROUD   *Paris*

Worked at rue Perdue 13 between 1838-42. (See Almanachs.)

BERTAULT   *Paris*

Shown in the 1816 Almanach as operating at St. Jacques 52.

BERTAULT, *Fils*   *Paris*

No doubt the son of the above, worked at the same address 1821–26.

BERTEL   *Paris*

Noted in the 1809 Almanach as established at rue des Vieux-Augustins 41.

BERTELAGE   *Le Mans*

His name, without date, was given to me by R. Paul Cordonnier, Keeper of the Library at Le Mans.

BERTHE, *Amand*   *Paris*

First appears in 1826 at Vieux Colombier 25, and later at Foin-St. Germain 17, where he apparently worked from 1832-35.

BERTHE, *Aîné*   *Paris*

Figures in the Almanachs at Haute-feuille 10 between 1821-26, but still active in 1829. (See Desc. II, 231.) The prefix "Aîné" is used by L. S. Le Normand in dedicating his book on binding, dated 1827, to Berthe.

BERTHE-NOEL   *Paris*

The Almanach entries cover the years 1832–38. Berthe-Noel was working in 1832 both at Hautefeuille 10 and at Battoir 2, and in 1838 at Jardinet 2–4. He earlier, in 1827, signed a dedication binding to his father-in-law, Berthe Aîné (see the Manuel du Relieur in the Paul Hirsch Collection, 1948). (See also Whitney Hoff, 587.)

BERTHE-ROMIEU   *Paris*

Worked at Hautefeuille 3, from 1840–42. By 1843, *Madame Berthe*, presumably his widow, was working at the same address, and from 1847–49 Berthe, possibly a son, was active also at the same address.

BERTHELLEMOT

The only notice of this binder is in Desc. II, 506, where a very rich mosaic binding of about 1824 is illustrated.

BERTHOUD, Louis   *Bordeaux*

Between 1789–92 at "sur le derrière des chartrons".

BERTHOUX   *Paris*

Worked at various addresses between 1821–32, as follows: Geoffroi l'Angevin 11 ('21); Chapon 2 ('26); Temple 43 ('32).

BERTHOUX, Mlle.   *Paris*

Probably the daughter of the above. Worked at Temple 43 from 1835 –36.

BERTIN

I have noticed his name during my studies, but have no details.

BERTRAND   *Paris*

Figures in the Almanachs at different addresses: Sept Voies 13 ('03); 25 ('09); 31 ('15). He may be the same, or related to the Jacques Bertrand, received as master-binder in 1767, and then living at Cour d'Albret, (Thoinan, p. 206). The Almanach Typographique cites him at rue Sept Voies in 1799.

BERTRAND   *Marseilles*

Active between 1838–46 at rue d'Aubagne; Chemin Neuf de la Magdelaine ('41); rue de la Providence 12 ('46).

BESCHEN   *Paris*

Active 1821–32. Addresses: St. Jacques 110 ('21); Marché Neuf 22 ('32).

BESNARD   *Paris*

Worked at rue Montmartre 39 in 1837 and at Hautefeuille 11 in 1840.

BESNIER   *Paris*

Appears to have had a long career at various addresses: Carmes 5 ('21); St. Jean-de-Beauvais 14 ('26); and 22 ('35); Galande 11 ('42). Was still working in 1847.

BEUGNER   *Paris*

Started in 1843 at Maçons-Sorbonne 1, and last appears at St. Jacques 67 in 1847.

BEUGNET, *Pierre*   *Lyons*

Worked at Grande rue Mercière in 1821.

BIBOLET   *Paris*

He may have started on his own as early as 1811. The 1826 Almanach shows him as established at rue de Grenelle 94, and at Passage Ste. Marie 10, and styling himself as pupil of Simier Père and binder to the Prince de Talleyrand. He figures in the Almanachs as late as 1842.

BIBOLET, *Veuve*   *Paris*

Appears at Passage Ste. Marie 10 in the 1847 Almanach.

BICHEBOIS   *Bordeaux*

In 1833 at Fossés de l'Indépendance 38, and at rue St. James 1836–39.

BIENVENU   *Paris*

Appears in 1797–98 as working at rue Neuve-St. Laurent 12.

BIGAUD, *François*   *Limoges*

Master-binder in 1789.

BIGOT

Figures in A. Poursin's Cat. of May 1949, Lot 71, as binding about
1824.

BILGER, *Louis*   *Strassburg*

Was at rue d'Echasses in 1824.

BILLONAUD   *Limoges*

At rue du Temple from 1836–48.

BILLOURDIN   *Paris*

Shown in the 1842 and 1843 Almanachs as working respectively at
Ste. Croix de la Bretonnière 5 and Boulevard du Temple 4.

BINAUX   *Paris*

Appears in the 1797 Paris Almanach at rue des Carmes 1.

BINOIS

D. d'E. reports a mosaic binding on an 1838 work in Cat. Wassermann, No. 1205.

BISIAUX, *Pierre-Joseph*   *Paris*

Worked between 1777–1801 (when he figures in the Paris
Almanach). His workshops were at Place Maubert in 1777; Foin
St. Jacques 32 in 1785; and Carmes 1 in 1798–1801.
One of the leading binders of the transition from the Monarchy
to the Directory; mentioned by Thoinan, p. 207, Gruel ('87), p. 54,
and ('05), p.34–35. Illustrations of his work can be seen in Schiff,
Nos. 121–2, 124, and 126–7; also in Whitney Hoff, No. 463.

BIZOUARD, *Charles-Pierre*   *Paris*

He is mentioned by Thoinan as having been received in 1774, and
as still working as late as 1822, always at the same address in rue des
Carmes 48. A binder of the same name figures in the 1803 Almanach

33

at Carmes 18, and from 1815–32 at No. 26. It is difficult to say if it is the same individual over the whole sixty odd years. A. M-C. quotes Bizouard in 1812 as "Relieur des Bibliothèques de S.M. l'Empereur".

BLACAS, *Aîné* *Paris*

First recorded in the Almanach of 1826 as at rue Bourbon 32, and then from 1832–43 at rue de Lille 32.

BLACHET, *Jacques-Nicolas II* *Paris*

Thoinan, p. 208, gives him as having been received into the community of binders in 1778 and having lived at rue Charretière. He mentions a Blachet in the Almanach Dauphin of 1777, and the Almanach de Paris of 1785, without mention of initials (if any) or place of working. He then goes on to say that the Almanach du Commerce of 1800 to 1803 mentions two Blachets, but again does not give their streets, much less the number therein. As regards the exact day and the month when each pre-Revolution binder was received, Thoinan seems, however, to cite these details with great precision, and I have therefore not repeated them in this work.

BLACHET *Paris*

Cited by Thoinan, p. 208, as mentioned by 1800–03 Almanachs. Worked at rue d'Ecosse in 1803.

BLACHET *Paris*

Cited by Thoinan with the above. Worked at Mt. St. Hilaire 11 from 1799–1803, and is styled "Aîné" by the 1799 Almanach Typographique.

BLACHET, *Jeune* *Paris*

Mentioned in 1799 Almanach Typographique at rue Charretière.

BLAIN, *Jean-François* *Paris*

Thoinan, p. 208, mentions him as active between 1765–90, without giving his authority for the statement.

BLAISE, *Charles* *Paris*

The Almanachs show him at rue Marais 17 bis from 1835, and at rue du Bac 68 from 1840–49. A copy of *Le Saphir*, 1832, in full morocco gilt in my own collection may have been bound in that year. He was an excellent craftsman.

BLAISE (*and gilder*) *Paris*

Working at rue de Seine 16 between 1832–40. (See relative Almanachs.)

BLAISE, *Jeune* *Paris*

D. d'E. quotes a binding (*c.* 1820) on a work dated 1813 with a paper label: A la Providence/ Blaise Jeune/ relieur/ Quai des Augustins/ a Paris.

BLAIZOT *Paris*

R.L.B. of New York states that he worked for Marie-Antoinette from about 1775 till the Queen's death.

BLANC *Paris*

Appears in Almanachs 1836–43 at Dupuis-Vendôme 9 ('36) and Tabletterie 9 ('43).

BLANC *Marseilles*

Worked at rue d'Aubagne in 1803–05 and had disappeared before 1812.

BLANCHARD *Paris*

Worked at rue d'Ecosse 8 between 1835–42.

BLANCHARD *Paris*

Cited in Lesné ('27), p. 214, as an "edge-gilder".

BLANDINEAU *Bordeaux*

At rue Ste. Hélène 7 ('33–'39) and rue de l'Archevêche 1 ('48).

BLANGIS *Paris*

Mentioned in Lesné ('27), p. 190, as only second to Pelicier as an "edge-gilder" by the acid method and also on p. 214.

BLEMOND *Limoges*

At rue du Verdurier from 1836–48.

BLONDEAU *Paris*

Given in the 1799 Almanach Typographique as at rue d'Ecosse.

BLONDEAU *Paris*

Noted by the Almanachs as working at St. Jacques 70 between 1815 and 1826.

BLONDEAU *Paris*

His sole appearance seems to be in the 1838 Almanach at rue St. Jean-de-Beauvais 16.

BLONDEAU *Paris*

Figures for the first time at the end of our period in 1847 at rue St. Jacques 30.

BLONDEL *Paris*

Appears in the 1838–40 Almanachs at Cour Harlay 17.

BLONDEL, *Mme.* *Paris*

Noted at Jérusalem 3 in 1842.

BLONDIN *Abbeville*

At rue des Lingers in 1826.

BLUMENTHAL *Paris*

Worked at Maçons 8 in 1847 and two years later at rue du Temple 13.

BLUMENTHAL *Paris*

Like the above, appears for the first time in 1847, but at Mouton 7.

BODET *Nantes*

At rue de la Fosse 40 in 1845.

BOEGLIN, *Antoine* *Lyons*

First noted in 1813 at Palais-Grillet 1 and last at rue Chalamont 2 in 1821.

BOEGNER *Paris*

Does not appear in the Almanachs, but seems to have worked at rue de la Harpe 21 about 1843. (See Whitney Hoff 599.)

BOERSCH *Paris*

Reported by R.L.B. as working 1826–36. For an example of his work see Bér. V, 279. Also Romb. 42/3// C. 274 on a work dated 1837. His address was 27 rue Louis-le-Grand. He signed with Valentin (*q.v.*) about 1833.

BOGETTI *Paris*

The only example of his work which has come to my notice is Desc. II, 214 (*c.* 1824). D. d'E. also quotes him as figuring in Cat. Schumann 411.

BOGILLOT *Nantes*

At rue du Soleil 1804–05.

BOHM, *Henry*

An example of his work (*c.* 1847) appears in Desc. II, 269.

BOILET *Paris*

A late binder of the period, who first appears in 1847 at rue de la Harpe 58.

BOISSEAU, *Antoine* *Paris*

Figures at Mont. St. Hilaire 14 in the Almanachs from 1803–10. The 1799 Almanach Typographique mentions a Boisseau*x* in the same street.

BOISSEL *Paris*

Entries in the Almanachs show him as working at rue Vieille du Temple 50 in 1809; No. 90 in 1815 and No. 88 in 1832 (the last entry). The Almanach Typographique of 1799 gives a binder of the same name in the rue Cossonnerie.

BOISSONET

The only example of his work which I have noticed is a half-calf binding on Desbordes-Valmore *Poésies* 2 vol. 1830 in Blaizot Cat. 298 No. 144.

BONFILS *Paris*

Shown in the 1835–49 Almanachs as at Roule 15. Specimens are listed in Maggs 661, 178 and Bér. III, 54.

BONNAIRE *Paris*

Figures in 1815–32 Almanachs as follows: Git-le-Cœur 5 (1815); Harpe 40 (1821); Battoir St. André 13 (1826). His work is illustrated in Sch. 306.

BONNARD

I have no information beyond his name.

BONNAUD, or BONNEAU *Paris*

Worked at rue St. Jacques 124 from 1824–36. (Almanachs.)

BORCK (also BORK, BORCQ, and BORCH) *Paris*

Started at Seine 27 in 1815, and later worked at Mathurins 1 from 1832–36.

BORCH, Mme. *Paris*

Mentioned in the 1847 Almanach as working at Mathurins 1.

BORDAS *Limoges*

Master-binder in 1789.

BOSC

The only specimen of his work known to me is in Béraldi Cat. III, No. 91, on a work dated 1833. The style approximates closely to that of the almost contemporary English binders Lewis and Dawson.

BOSQUI *Marseilles*

Started work in 1803 at Montée du Grand Hospice and was later at Place du Palais de Justice between 1812–15.

BOTHEY

Nothing known beyond his name.

BOTTIER, (?Louis-François)   *Paris*

Was the son-in-law of J. B. Duplanil I (see Thoinan, p. 271). Worked at Sept Voies 27 between 1798–1801. See also Gruel ('05) II, p. 39. He may be Louis-François, son of François.

BOTTIER, Joseph   *Paris*

Appears in the 1798–1803 Almanachs at rue Bordet 29. See Thoinan, p. 209, and Gruel ('05), p. 36.

BOTTIER   *Paris*

His connection with the other binders of the same name and period is not clear. He is noted as having worked in 1832 at rue d'Ecosse 8.

BOTTIER, Fils   *Paris*

Worked at St. Etienne-des-Grès 12 from 1821–32. He may well have been the *Bothier* mentioned by Lesné ('27) on p. 306. Sch. 304 illustrates a specimen of his work. See also Romb. 46/ c. 416.

BOTTIER, Nestor   *? Paris*

The only specimen of his work known to me is a half-morocco binding signed in full on the spine (about 1836) in my own collection. Small tools and bold diagonal straight lines. His work was apparently much valued by his contemporaries.

BOULANGER, Pierre-Jules-Bernard   *Paris*

Mentioned by Thoinan, p. 210, as working from 1776–90, and located in 1785 at rue du Petit-Pont. He seems to have been a gilder as well, and also a publisher of almanachs of the current type. See Gruel ('87), p. 58 and ('05), p.37.

BOURBIER   *Amiens*

At rue Henri IV 21 in 1826.

BOURDEUX, *et Fils*

Item 93 in the Catalogue of the London (1948) Exhibition "Thousand Years of French Books", Buffon. Hist. Nat. 1749–1804, is stated to be bound in contemporary German full calf, and to bear the above's ticket in French as "booksellers by appt. to the Prussian Court". No indication of place of work, but they were probably French binders by origin.

BOUROCH

Probably worked about 1832. See Bér. III, 438, and Desc. II, 113.

BOURREAU   *Bordeaux*

At Cours de Tourny 62 (’33–’39): 43 (’48).

BOURRELIER (BOURLIER)   *Paris*

Thoinan, p. 212, gives him as working at Quai des Augustins in 1789. According to R.L.B. he was active between 1785–1800.

BOUTAULT   *Paris*

According to Thoinan, p. 212, three members of this family worked at rue des Amandiers, as follows: Louis-Antoine from 1768, Guillaume-Marie from 1769, and Nicolas II from 1774. Boutault, Père et Fils, and another existed till 1801. One Boutault appears at Amandiers 3 in the 1803 Almanach. A Bou*teau*, Père and a Bou*teau*, Fils appear in the 1799 Almanach Typographique at rue des Amandiers.

BOUTIGNY   *Paris*

Binder to the University. First noted in 1835 at rue St. Jacques 122 and last at Grès 10 in 1847. The leading exponent of the rocaille school of binding; much of his work was done anonymously for publishers.

BOUTIN   *Paris*

Worked at rue Jérusalem 3 in 1847–49.

BOUTOILLE-PETITOT   *Lille*

Addresses: Place du Théâtre 27 (’43); rue de la Quennette 7 (’48).

BOUVET, François   *Lyons*

Worked at Grande rue Mercière 64 in 1832.

BOUVET   *Marseilles*

Started at rue St. Jaume in 1812 and was later at Place du Cul-de-
Bœuf between 1813–1815.

BOYENVAL   *Paris*

Noted in the 1838–42 Almanachs at Temple 36 and St. Jacques 27.
(See Cat. Rousseau-Girard No. 10/49.)

BOZERIAN, Joseph C.   *Paris*

His Christian names are uncertain, as Gumachian XII, 332, quoted
a book published by *Je. Cl.* Bozérian, *relieur*, dated 1801.
He appears to have worked from 1795–1810 and, according to
Bér. Rel., exhibited in 1801. I have been unable to trace any printed
binder's ticket, but a MS. note on No. 257 of Marie-Louise's sale at
Sotheby's July 26 1933, gives his address as 33 Quai des Augustins.
This is confirmed by a note in the 1795 2 vol. ed. of Lafontaine's *Contes*
printed by P. Didot, Aîné, which states that it can be bought chez
Bozérian at 33 Quai des Augustins. It shows Bozérian was probably
also at that date acting as a bookseller. He is also quoted in the
1803 Paris Almanach.
A quite ordinary binding in my possession on Serieys: *Tables Chrono-
logiques* ('03) is typical of his hack bindery work.
A general review of his work and that of Bozérian Jeune is contained
in the preface to this work. Examples of his finer productions can
be seen in all the standard catalogues of the 1789–1815 period.

BOZERIAN, Jeune   *Paris*

Here again I have been unable to trace his Christian names (though
Bér. Rel. I, p. 34, gives his initial as F.), nor his exact relationship
to the elder Bozérian (possibly his brother), with whom he seems
to have worked in close contact for some four or five years, at any
rate on the wholesale bindery side. Béraldi, Reliure au XIXe, gives
his years of activity as 1805–18, and he appears in the Almanachs,
at 31 rue de Tournon from 1809–16. On the other hand, Thouvenin
states that he started working with **Bozérian Jeune** as early as 1802.

An attempt to evaluate his position as a binder, as well as that of the elder Bozérian, has been made by the writer in the introduction to this work. Dibden attacked him violently; Lesné, while defending French as opposed to English binding against Dibden, had little good to say of the younger Bozérian; and finally Thouvenin treats him as a wholesale massacrer of books. It is probably not unfair to say that he was a competent hack binder on a large scale, with no bibliographic sense especially as far as cutting margins, sewing, permanency of his work, etc., were concerned.

BOZERIAN and LEFEBVRE   *Paris*

The history of this combination is obscure. We do not know if the Bozérian in question were the elder or the younger. Their co-operation may have lasted from 1796–1816. Suffice it to say that this combination of two or three rather second-class binders could on occasion produce felicitous results which none of them, working separately, could create. (See Sch. II, 171.)

BRADEL, *Family*   *Paris*

Following the example of Thoinan, I do not feel that any useful purpose would be served by an attempt to disentangle the different Bradels of the 1789–1848 period. A basis for anyone who may wish to undertake the task can be found on p. 221 of Thoinan's work.

BRAND

The only specimen of this extremely rare binder known to me appears in Béraldi Cat. III, 411. In style it approximates to the work of Hering and Purgold.

BRASSY

Possibly worked about 1823. See Rombaldi Annuaire 42/3// A. 824.

BRAU   *Nantes*

First at rue Notre Dame ('17) and finally at rue Bourlon in 1825.

BRAULIET   *Paris*

See Chezaud.

BRAUN, J.   *Strassburg*

Worked at Dentelles 30 in 1846.

BRAYES   *Paris*

Son-in-law of J. B. 1er Duplanil. Possibly only an assistant. See Thoinan, p. 271.

BREMOND, *Louis*   *Marseilles*

Worked at rue Vacon 45 between 1846–48.

BREQUET

I have no information beyond his name.

BRIDE   *Paris*

Appears in the Almanachs as follows: St. Jacques 104 ('37); St. Jean de Beauvais 16 ('38); Bièvre 31 ('40).

BRIGANDAT   *Paris*

He appears in the Almanachs from 1835 when he was at rue Neuve St. Augustin 10 till 1843, when he moved to rue Coquenard 54. He may, however, have been working as early as 1825. Illustrations of his excellent binding appear in Gum. XII, 361; Maggs, 661/132; and Sch. III, 307.

BRIOTET

I have no details regarding him.

BRISSART

About 1837. See Rombaldi Ann, 42/3. C. 288.

BROCHOT   *Paris*

Makes his only appearance in the Almanachs in 1842 at Cloître St. Benoit 4.

BROCHOT, *Fils*   *Paris*

Noted at Mathurins 3 from 1840–42.

BROCHOT, *Veuve*　　　　　　　　　　　　　　　　　　　　*Paris*

　　Appears in the 1843 Almanach at Mathurins 3 and Cloître St. Benoit 4.

BROD, H.　　　　　　　　　　　　　　　　　　　　　*Strassburg*

　　At Jeu-des-Enfants 12 in 1846.

BRUYER　　　　　　　　　　　　　　　　　　　　　　*Paris*

　　His name is followed in each of the 1842–47 Almanachs which I
have seen by the words "C.F. 1834–39", which I am unable to
explain. He worked at rue St. Martin 249.

BRUYERE *Jérome*　　　　　　　　　　　　　　　　　　　*Lyons*

　　Worked at Grenelle 91, 1810; Confort 5 ('13); and 10 ('32–'42).

BUFFAT　　　　　　　　　　　　　　　　　　　　　　*Paris*

　　Carried on at Cordiers St. Jacques 10 from 1821–26.

BUGNET　　　　　　　　　　　　　　　　　　　　　　*Paris*

　　Noted in 1843 at Bucherie 11.

BUISSON, *Fils*　　　　　　　　　　　　　　　　　　　*Paris*

　　Appears in the 1803 Almanach at Percée 7.

BUIZARD　　　　　　　　　　　　　　　　　　　　　*Paris*

　　His only appearance, to my knowledge, is in the 1809 Almanach at
Michodière 4.

BUJADOUX　　　　　　　　　　　　　　　　　　　　*Paris*

　　Seems to have started at Montagne Ste. Geneviève 52 in 1838, and
to have moved in 1843 to No. 61 in the same street.

BULLIARD, *François*　　　　　　　　　　　　　　　　　*Dijon*

　　At 48 rue des Godrans in 1848.

BULPIAU

　　I have failed to trace any details.

BUNEL   *Paris*

Noted at Pavé St. André 9 in 1842 and at Port Mahon 5 in the
following year.

BUNETIER   *Paris*

Recorded in the Almanachs at rue de la Harpe 58 between 1842–49.
Seen as a signature on a full calf binding in Paris, February 1950.

BUQUAI   *Paris*

Address: Bièvre 31, 1847–49.

BURNIER

See Firmin Didot Cat. 1881 No. 531. Still binding in 1867.

BURTON, Veuve   *Paris*

Appears in the Almanach Typographique of 1799 at rue Amandiers.

BUSSEUIL, Aîné   *Nantes*

At Place du Pilori, 1804–08.

BUSSIERE   *Paris*

Quoted by 1842 Almanach at Galande 47.

CABANIS

Lesné ('27), p. 40, refers to him as sewing his bindings in the Dutch
style, and classes him with Bradel as an inferior imitator of foreign
workmanship.

CABANY, St. Maurice, Veuve.   *Paris*

Cited as working at Ste. Avoie 57 in 1847.

CADY   *Paris*

Mentioned in the 1809 Almanach as a binder and gilder working at
Plâtre-St. Jacques.

CAILLIBOTHIN   *Paris*

Lesné ('27), pp. 107 and 306, mentions his ultra-rapid work and
evidently had a poor opinion of his products.

CALLI, *Augustin*   *Paris*

He is only known to me by a reference in Thoinan, p. 223, where he is said to have worked between 1780–90.

CALLIER, *Françoise (née Fixon)*   *Paris*

She signed a Vernis-Martin binding on *Trois Comédies* by C. G. Etienne.

CALONNE   *Paris*

According to the 1843 Almanach, was then working at rue St. Honoré 216.

CAMILLE

Only his name is known to me.

CAMPION, *Fils*   *Lille*

At rue des Sept-Sauts 5 between 1832–38.

CAMUS, *Mme.*   *Paris*

Worked at Vieille Boucherie 29 in 1803.

CANON   *Paris*

A binder and gilder who appears in the !Almanachs from 1797–1836, always at St. Jean de Beauvais 29. Lesné ('27), p. 214, states that he specialised in edge-gilding. The only quotation of his work which I have been able to trace is in Rombaldi's Annuaire for 1947/ C. 593.

CANU   *Paris*

Makes an appearance in the 1803 Almanach at rue de la Harpe 240.

CAPE   *Paris*

Curiously, his name does not appear in any of the Almanachs of the period, but I have in my collection an excellent half-calf binding on D'Arlincourt's Ismailie ('28), which is a first-rate piece of work of that date, and a full calf binding on Beranger's Works dated ('37), also strictly contemporaneous. The latter has blind-stamped sides exactly similar to those on a binding by Libermann (*q.v.*), possibly earlier in date, on a book dated 1828. Capé is an example of a binder who did his best work at the start, and never reached the same level in his later and more prosperous old age.

Mr. Ellic Howe, 5 Thurloe Close, London S.W., possesses a specimen book of leathers and papers, bound by Capé about 1840, and inscribed as follows: "Cet album d'échantillons a été composé par Capé, *relieur du Roi*, au Louvre pour moi L. HUGOT (Conservateur des Bibliothèques Royales) qui le conserve comme un souvenir de mon cher Capé". Interesting specimens are: Veau antique (highly surfaced); veau solitaire (?); papier ombré (marbled); chiné (highly surfaced); d'Annonay (blotted effect), etc.

CARNEVILLIER — Paris

The 1832 Almanach reports him as working at rue St. Honoré 123.

CARNEVILLIER, *Veuve* — Paris

She is mentioned in the 1840–42 Almanach as working at rue Montmartre 26.

CARON, *Veuve* — Chartres

Working in 1841.

CAROUET — Paris

Appears at rue St. Jacques 152 in 1821.

CARRE, *Pierre* — Paris

Seems to have started work in 1776, and to have been at Mt. Hilaire 14 in 1797, and subsequently at Amandiers 17 from 1803–32. See Almanachs and Thoinan, p. 224, also Almanach Typographique 1799.

CARRE — Paris

Lesné ('27), p. 214, states that he was essentially a gilder, but he also seems to have bound. His addresses, as given in the Almanachs, are: Mazarine 62 ('21); rue Neuve des Petits-Champs 97 ('26); Jacob 4 ('32); 36 ('37–'43).

CARRET, *Antoine*   *Lyons*

At Bâtiment Claustral des Jacobins 79 ('10); 5 ('13–'16).

CARRET, *Claude*   *Lyons*

His address was Thomassin 18 in 1842.

CARRET, *Pierre-Benoit*   *Lyons*

He worked at Tupin 2 between 1821–42.

CARROLL   *Paris*

He may have started as early as 1822. His name appears in 1832–40
Almanachs at Neuve-Coquenard 18. My own collection contains:
Wagre: Prisonnier de Cabrera ('28), in a full binding with the arms,
etc., of the Duchesse de Berry. A specimen of his work is also
illustrated in Maggs' Cat. 661, No. 117.

CARTAULT (*or* CARTAUT)   *Paris*

Figures at Plâtre St. Jacques 24 in 1838 and at St. Jacques 38 in 1847.

CASSASSUS

May have bound as early as 1801, but certainly between 1835–40.
His bindings have a rich square effect. See Bér. Vente III, 68, and
Desc. II, 27, and a purple calf binding on Biblia Sacra, 1827, in my
own collection with interesting ecclesiastical emblems on spine.
I have been unable to trace where he worked, but the fact that books
bound by him often carry the labels of Rouen booksellers such as
Fleury and Edet Jeune may be significant.

CASTELN(E)AU   *Paris*

The Almanachs report him as working at Noyers 8 between 1838
and 1847.

CASTERA   *Bordeaux*

At rue de la Merci 13 in 1848.

CASTILLON   *Bordeaux*

Près St. Michel in 1789.

CAUMONT, *Cte. Auguste-Marie de* *London*

This French nobleman was born at Villers-sur-Aumale on October 28, 1743, and died at Derchigny, Arrondissement Dieppe in 1839. There is nothing to show that he had any experience in binding before emigrating from France, nor is there any evidence that he bound after returning to France about 1814–15. It is accordingly not a matter for astonishment that his work is practically unknown in France. In England, however, where he worked for just over twenty years from 1790 onwards, he is considered a very great binder, in an age when English bookbinding was temporarily at a high level, and actually far ahead of contemporary French binding. (See Thouvenin Aîné.)

A full account of his career is to be found in Thoinan, p. 224 *et seq.* He appears to have commenced his activities as early as 1790 (A. M-S. 361) at 3 Portland Street, then to have moved to 1 Frith Street, Soho Square, and lastly to 39 Gerrard Street, Soho.

His work, though he enjoyed very distinguished patronage, is by no means common. I am lucky to have an excellent specimen of his later period, with the Frith Street label. It is a first-rate vellum binding, with gilt and light blue ornamentation, on J. Wilson Croker's *Battles of Talavera*, 1810, in the Edwards of Halifax style. It is a dedication copy from the author to the Hon. Mrs. Perceval, the wife of the Prime Minister assassinated at the House of Commons a year or two later. Strangely enough, it is badly "squared"; perhaps a sign of the amateur.

CAUTELEUX (*sometimes misspelt CANTELEUX*) *Paris*

He seems to have been active from 1803–36. His first address seems to have been Sept-Voies 6, from which he moved to No. 11 in 1809, and finally to No. 16 in 1832.

CAUVIN *Lille*

The town Almanach for 1789 notes him at rue de Tenremonde.

CAVALIER *Marseilles*

Active 1803–38, first at rue Beausset, and then from 1813 at rue des Auffiers.

CAZEAU, *Eugène*

Maggs 661/224 illustrates a binding by the above, who appears to style himself as a gilder, and to date his binding 1848; the volume is the 1844 illustrated Perrotin *Notre Dame*.

CELARD   *Paris*

Figures at rue de Bac 91 from 1842–43.

CELLIAT

Again just a name.

CELLIER (*or SELLIER*)

Active about 1803. (See Whitney-Hoff, 670.)

CERF *et* NAXARA   *Bordeaux*

At rue Royale 16 in 1833–39.

CHABANNE   *Paris*

Quoted in the 1842–47 Almanachs at Coquillière 1.

CHABAUT   *Paris*

Noted at Bordet 29 in 1803.

CHABOT   *Paris*

The 1797–98 Almanach mentions him at Séverin 143.

CHABRILLA   *Bordeaux*

At rue Porte Dijeaux in 1839.

CHABROL   *Limoges*

In 1836 he was at rue du Canard. In 1846 there were two binders of this name, one at rue Puy-Vieille-Monnaie and the other at rue du Clocher.

CHAECK

I know no specimen of his work.

CHALUT

I can supply no information regarding him.

CHAMAISON, B.   *Bordeaux*

Rue Bouffard 4 ('33); rue des Remparts 15 ('36–'39); rue Castillon ('48).

CHAMPY   *Paris*

The 1797 Almanach mentions a binder of this name at Charretière 7, and that of 1803 one of similar name at St. Jacques, chez le Peaussier.

CHAMPY   *Paris*

This binder, who may be the same as the above, worked at St. Séverin 14 in 1816, and later at Parcheminerie 7 from 1826–36.

CHANINEL   *Paris*

Worked at rue Argenteuil 37 from 1838–47, when he moved to No. 51 in the same street.

CHAPPUIS   *Paris*

Quoted in the 1799 Almanach Typographique at rue Christine.

CHAPRON (*and DE BEAUVAIS, q.v.*)   *Paris*

This binder of distinction, whose only address seems to have been rue de Wertinghen 10, Abbaye St. Germain, started work possibly about 1800, and continued certainly till 1812, and possibly later. He at first co-operated with Alexandre de Beauvais, and this association certainly continued till 1808 (see Sch. III, 230). By 1809, however, a split had evidently occurred, and de Beauvais had his own label at rue de l'Observance 7 (see Sch. III, 234), which he continued to use till at least 1818 (see O. C., Lourdoueix: *Folies de Siècle*). Chapron apparently did not issue a label of his own after parting company with de Beauvais, contenting himself with erasing the latter's name in ink (see Sch. III, 231–3).

CHAPRON, V.   *Paris*

His name appears in the Almanachs, first at Seine 30 in 1826 and later at Quai Conti 5 in 1842–47. My own collection contains a blonde calf binding, signed on the base of the spine and with strictly contemporary Indian ink drawings on each side.

CHARLES   *Limoges*

At rue Manigne between 1846–48.

CHARON   *Paris*

Evidence from books of reference gives him as working between
1836 and 1843 at St. Louis-le-Grand 33. A specimen of his work is
illustrated in Barthou Vol. I, No. 149, Plate XXIV.

CHARPENTIER   *Paris*

Appears in the 1847 Almanach at rue Dauphin 12.

CHARTIER   *Angers*

At rue Chaperonnière in 1848.

CHARTIER   *Paris*

First noticed in 1838 at Oratoire du Louvre 12, and later at rue des
Deux Ecus 7 in 1842.

CHASSAGNOT   *Paris*

The Almanachs record him first at Foin St. Jacques 30 in 1832, and
then at Parcheminerie 2 from 1835–43.

CHATAIGNER   *Bordeaux*

"A l'Académie des Sciences" 1789–92.

CHATELIER   *Nantes*

At Haute Grande-Rue in 1843.

CHAUDESAYGUES   *Paris*

Worked at St. Etienne-des-Grès 12 from 1836–47.

CHAULIN

No details are known to me.

CHAUMONT, *Antoine*   *Paris*

Thoinan, p. 228, gives a substantial account of the Chaumont family,
but makes no specific mention of Antoine, one of the most important
of the 1800–20 binders.

He first appears about 1797–98, and the following are his addresses: Foin 260 ('98); 209 ('03); Foin St. Jacques 18, Hotel de la Reine Blanche ('15). His last mention in the Almanachs is in 1821.

My own specimen of his work: *Martialis Epigrammata* 1701 in full morocco gilt from the Beckford-Hamilton Collection is worthy to rank with the best plain work of the Derôme family. Good illustrations of his work are to be found in the Schiff Catalogue II, Nos. 115, 118, and 119. In No. 118 he styles himself binder to the Institut de France.

CHAUMONT, *Jeune*   *Paris*

Quoted in the 1803 Almanach as working at Pierre-Sarrazin 5.

CHAUMONT   *Paris*

Two binders of this name were working between 1821–26, one at rue d'Ecosse 6 and the other at Place Sorbonne 3 in 1821 and at Marais 13 in 1826.

CHAUVEL   *Paris*

He worked at Noyers 15 from 1842–44.

CHAUVIN   *Paris*

The Almanachs 1832–47 refer to him at rue Sabot 4.

CHAVANT, *Jean-Marie*   *Lyons*

The Lyons Guide for 1842 gives his address as Tupin 22.

CHENTRIER   *Angers*

At rue Baudrière in 1840.

CHENU, *Jacques II*   *Paris*

Thoinan, p. 229, mentions him as still alive in 1790, which would bring him into our scope. He was received as a master-binder in 1759, and lived in rue Charretière.

CHENU   *Paris*

A gilder as well as a binder. He worked from 1826–42 at various addresses as follows: St. Hilaire 6 ('26); St. J. de Beauvais 16 ('32); Carmes 5 ('38); St. J. de Beauvais 30 ('40).

CHERET   *Paris*

At Pavée St. André 14 from 1836–42.

CHERONNET

A portfolio dated 1806 and bearing the above binder's name was noticed by me in Paris in May 1949.

CHESLE (*see LEMONNIER*)   *Paris*

This "gauffrer" of plates for blind-stamping bindings lived at Montagne-Ste. Geneviève about 1825. See Béraldi Rel. II, Plate 56. In the 1823 Paris Exhibition the firm was styled as Lemonnier & Chesle.

CHEVALIER   *Paris*

Worked at rue Voltaire 12 from 1832–36.

CHEVALIER-DUFEY   *Paris*

Noted at Passage Dauphine in 1847.

CHEZAUD & BRAULIET   *Paris*

Mentioned in the Almanachs from 1842 at Tissanderie 23, and from 1843 at Verrerie 55 till 1849. A specimen of his work is illustrated in Béraldi Cat. V, No. 208.

CHICHEREAU, *Jean*   *Paris*

Given by Thoinan, p. 229, as working at rue des Amandiers 18 from 1776–1803, at which latter date he appears in the Almanach.

CHICHEREAU, *Pierre*   *Paris*

Thoinan, p. 229, says that he was also received in 1776 and lived at Mont-St. Hilaire. From 1797–1803 he appears to have lived at Ecosse 6.

CHICHEREAU (*or CHICHEROUX*)   *Paris*

First figures in the Almanachs at Foin St. Jacques 10 in 1821; moved to No. 63 about 1840 and to St. Jean-de-Beauvais 11 in 1847.

CHILLIAT   *Paris*

Though the only references to him in the Almanachs are for 1815 (rue St. Jacques 2) and 1816 (Parcheminerie 2), he probably worked over a longer period. Specimens of his work are illustrated in Maggs 661/44 and Sch. III, 286. I possess a binding very similar to the latter on a 3 volume edition of Montaigne's *Essais* 1559.

CHOPPART   *Marseilles*

Worked at rue des Templiers 17 between 1826–35.

CHRETIEN   *Bordeaux*

At rue du Hâ 35 in 1848.

CLAMOUZE   *Bordeaux*

At rue de Cahernan 6 ('36) (as Clamouze & Reynaudie); rue Pas-St. George 3 ('39); and (alone) at rue des Bahutiers 20 ('48).

CLEBERT   *Nantes*

At rue Beau-Soleil in 1808.

CLEMENT   *Orleans*

At rue des Petits-Souliers in 1832 and rue des Grisons in 1846.

CLERET   *Paris*

Figures in the Almanachs 1826–49, first at Pavée St. André 14, and latterly in 1847 at Hauteville 98.

CLERGET   *Paris*

A gauffrer working about 1843.

CLOSON   *Aix*

At rue des Grands-Carmes 21 in 1822.

CLOSS   *Paris*

Was first at Boucher 14 in 1838, and then from 1840–49 at St. Germain-l'Auxerrois 66. I have a competent, but rather dull specimen of his work.

CLUZEAU, *Caroline*   *Bayonne*

 Worked between 1840–50 at Argenterie 12 as bookseller, stationer, and binder.

COCHEU   *Tours*

 Figures in Cat. Mouravit No. 512.

CODBAT, *François (and bookseller)*   *Metz*

 Born at Metz May 24, 1822. Set up at rue de l'Evêché and later at rue de la Tête d'Or, where he worked till his death on September 22, 1888.

COLAS   *Orleans*

 Noted at rue des Minimes in 1807.

COLAS   *Orleans*

 Probably the son of the above; was at rue des Fauchets in 1832 and at rue Pavée, à la Bibliothèque, in 1846.

COLIBERT   *Paris*

 The 1803 Almanach gives him as working at rue de la Harpe 467 in 1803.

COLIN-BELLEROCHE   *Paris*

 According to the Almanachs, worked at Thibautode 18 in 1835–36.

COLLARD

 No particulars on record.

COLLET   *Paris*

 At St. Jean-de-Beauvais 15 in 1838 and at Mont-St. Hilaire 14 in 1847.

COLLIBERT   *Paris*

 Quoted as a sewer and gatherer from 1815–16 at Parcheminerie 2.

COLOMBIN

 Only name has been noted.

COLON(N)IER   *Angers*

   At rue St. Aubin from 1831–48.

COMELARAN   *Paris*

   In 1832 he worked at rue Seine 6; and in 1836 moved to No. 9, where
   he worked till 1843. Desc. II, 408, illustrates a specimen of his work.

CONSIDERANT   *Paris*

   Makes a brief appearance at Amandiers 13 in 1832.

CONSIDERANT, *Veuve*   *Paris*

   Presumably the widow of the above, worked at the same address
   from 1835–36.

CONSTANT   *Limoges*

   At rue du Verdurier in 1836; and at rue Puy-Vieille-Monnaie
   1846–48.

CONTAL   *Nancy*

   No details available.

CONTE, *Père*   *Toulouse*

   Address in 1838:—à l'Université.

CONTE, *Fils*   *Toulouse*

   Addresses: rue du Seneschal ('38); rue Peyrolières 17 ('47); rue
   Chaude ('48).

CORDIER, *François*   *Marseilles*

   At rue Caisserie 52 between 1846–48.

CORFMAT   *Paris*

   According to the Almanachs, he first appears at St. Jacques 110 in
   1840, where he continued till 1843. He was probably active for
   considerably longer, and a binder of the same name appears at
   St. Jacques 124 in 1849. An example of his work is illustrated in
   Whitney Hoff 592, and I have in my own collection a nice calf binding
   in the Bonfils style with dedication by Queen Marie-Amélie dated
   9th January 1845.

CORFMAT   *Paris*

There are a number of other binders of the same name and approximate period, whom it is difficult to place exactly. Thus there is a second Corfmat in the 1842 Almanach at Galande 37; an E. Corfmat, Jeune at St. Séverin 16 in 1847–49, and yet another at Zacharie 9 in 1849. I have an excellent straight-lined calf binding on a work dated 1834 which might well be contemporary, and another signed "Corfmat, J."

CORN, T.   *Strassburg*

At Place du Dôme 24 in 1846.

CORNU   *Nantes*

Worked from 1817 to 1848 at rue Suffren.

CORNU   *Paris*

He figures in the 1799 Almanach Typographique, otherwise his only appearance in the Almanachs seems to be in 1803 at Amandiers 21. Though Lesné ('27), p. 340, notes him as comparatively unknown, he was presumably still alive about 1827.

COSSARD   *Paris*

Appears in 1803 at Mont-St. Hilaire 1.

COSSE   *Paris*

Binder to the Artillery and Military Academy Libraries from 1842–47. First address: Filles du Calvaire 29 and from 1843 Boulevard du Temple 16.

COSTEY, *Frères*

Rousseau-Girard's Cat. 12/49 quotes a contemporary half-binding on the 1823 (Dalibon) Rabelais.

COTELLE (*and gilder*)   *Paris*

The 1843 Almanach mentions him at Garancière 3.

COTHON-CHARBONNAIS, *Mme.*   *Paris*

At Christine 1 from 1847–49.

COTTY, *Jean-Etienne* *Paris*

Thoinan mentions on p. 234 that he was received in 1776, and lived at rue Char(re)tière. Subsequently he apparently lived from about 1799–1820 at Mont-St. Hilaire 1, though the only reference to him which I have traced in the Almanachs is in 1799 and 1803. Lesné places him among the good binders of the second category of his time.

COTTY, *Demoiselles* *Paris*

Sch. 226 illustrates a probably contemporary binding by the above on Bernis' works 1803.

COTTY, *Frères* *Paris*

? 1811.

COULON *Paris*

His first address in 1842 was Joubert 9, and from 1847 Thiroux 8.

COULOUGNAN *Montpellier*

Binder to the Faculty of Medicine. Worked in 1835 at rue Petit Scel and later at rue des Esquilles.

COUOT *Toulouse*

At rue St. Antoine du T. 32 ('47–'48).

COURTEVAL *Paris*

One of the greatest binders of his day; he worked from about 1796–1836, and executed much of his work himself. Thoinan, p. 234, refers to his "gaufrages", and to his marbled calf, but they are unknown to me. His best bindings, made before 1815, show much delicate classical work. Specimens of his work are illustrated in Sch. II, 189–200; Desc. I, 22; and Gum. 335. Also Rahir VI, 2018. My own specimens of his work are a plain and workmanlike calf binding on the ('04) edition of *Poésies de Clotilde*, and an excellent example of pointillé-backed morocco binding on a 1695 Horace. His first address was Carmes 1, and later ('09) at No. 5, to which he often altered his label in ink.

COURTHELLEMONT

COURTOIS   *Paris*

Worked from 1826–43 at the following addresses: St. Jacques 124 ('26); Cimetière St. André 10 ('36); St. Jacques 104 ('38).

COUSIN, *Germain*   *Paris*

Thouvenin, 234, dates his activity from 1750–90.

COUTIL   *Paris*

Makes an appearance in the 1809 Almanach at Mont-St. Hilaire 6.

COUTTENIER   *Lille*

From 1840–48 at rue J. J. Rousseau 52.

CRANSARD   *Orleans*

At rue de la Lionne in 1846.

CREUSET   *Paris*

Active 1832–43. Addresses: St. André des Arts 9 ('32); Macon 10 ('38); Huchette 29 ('42).

CUIGNET, J. B.   *Lille*

Addresses: Place de l'Arsenal 4 ('29); rue de l'Arc 23 ('36); rue J. J. Rousseau 2 ('42).

CUISINIER (see *DELFORTRY*)   *Lille*

First at Grande-Chaussée 37 ('42); then rue du Curé St. Etienne 13 ('43–'48).

CULEMBOURG   *Paris*

Lesné ('27), pp.99 and 241, mentions him as a skilful engraver of binders' tools.

CURMER, L.   *Paris*

Though bindings about 1844 often bear his name, I am doubtful if his firm ever executed them.

DAMEL, François (and second-hand bookseller)   *Metz*

First established Place Croix-Outre-Moselle; then in 1809 at rue du Pont-St. Georges. Died September 5, 1825, aged 68.

DAMET   *Limoges*

Was at rue du Temple in 1836 and at rue du Consulat in 1848.

DAMOTTE   *Paris*

A designer of plates, tools, etc. His work is illustrated in Maggs 661/284 under date of 1852. It is probable, but not certain, that he was active before 1848.

DANOIS   *Paris*

Mentioned between 1809–16 at Rempart 11.

DANSARD   *Paris*

Appears in the 1839 Almanach at Mathurins 21.

DANZANVILLIERS   *Paris*

First appears at Carmes 15 in 1797 and then at No. 32, 1809–15. (See Olivier No. 2500–1 and Jean Coulet's Cat. December ('48), No. 438: Mariana. Hist. Gen. de España.) He seems to have been working as late as 1830.

DANZANVILLIERS, Fils   *Paris*

Quoted in the 1821 Almanach as Carmes 32, and then at No. 23 in 1836–47.

DARGENS, Joseph (and bookseller)   *Metz*

Born at Pontigy (Moselle) April 7, 1822; worked at Fournirue and died December 12, 1890.

DARRAS   *Amiens*

At Jeunes Mâtins 12 in 1826.

DARROUX   *Toulouse*

Worked at rue de la Baruthe in 1848.

DAUPHIN, Pierre — *Lyons*

The only authentic date with regard to this well-known binder which I have traced is in the *Nouvel Indicateur de Lyons* for 1832, when he was working at Petit-David 5. The many bindings of his listed in Maggs 661 appear to indicate that he may have been working already about ten years earlier.

DAUVERGNE, *Veuve* — *Paris*

See Gruel ('05), p. 55. She succeeded her husband Nicolas Rémi in 1789 and there also seems to have been a son active at the same date. Mme. Dauvergne was the heiress of E. Isoré (*q.v.*).

DAUVIN — *Paris*

After commencing work at Mont-St. Hilaire 2 in 1838, he moved to St. Jean-de-Beauvais 14 in 1840, where he was still working in 1849.

DEBALSKI (*or DEBELSKI*) — *Paris*

Recorded at Samson 9 from 1847–49.

DEBAUSSEAUX — *Paris*

A. M-S. 361 gives him as "Binder of the Imperial Library". His address from 1797–1815 was Mont-St. Hilaire 14.

DEBECOURT

Only his name is known to me.

DEBES — *Paris*

Appears in the Almanachs at Fosses-St. Germain 5 from 1840–49, but may have been active before that date. His work is illustrated in Desc. II, 268, and also quoted in Bér. Cat. III, 303 and 322.

DECAUME — *Paris*

The Almanach Typographique of 1799 quotes him at rue d'Ecosse.

DEBOISSEAU

Lesné ('27), p. 107, speaks of him with respect as being in the Derôme, Bradel, Chaumont class, but I have been unable to trace him.

DECHAUMONT   *Paris*

Noted in 1835 at Place Eccle de Médecine 12.

DECHAUMONT, L. N. (and gilder)   *Paris*

Appears in the 1821–26 Almanachs at rue de la Harpe 78.

DECHAUMONT, Père et Fils   *Paris*

Makes an appearance in 1847 at Ponthieu 17.

DECLE   *Paris*

First in the late Empire at Place de Jéna 8 (see Kundig Cat. June '48). Later he was apparently a binder to the King, and received a Medal of Honour in 1823. His address was then Roule 15, and he was active to 1826. He may have been succeeded by Vinet, who worked at the same address in 1827.

DEFAYE   *Limoges*

At rue Pont St. Martial in 1836.

DEFODY   *Angers*

Worked at rue des Poêliers ('31); Place St. Martin ('41); rue St. Laud ('48).

DEFORGE, Isidore   *Paris*

A binder who is famous for his own binding, and also from the fact that his daughter married the first of the three successive Gruels, the latest of whom still survives (May 1949). As a personal artist, it is extremely difficult, from want of material, to estimate his value. He figures in the Almanachs for the long period 1809–49. His addresses during the period were: Duphot 12 ('09); 24 ('15); Plâtre St. Jacques 20 ('36); Richepanse 9 ('40); St. Honoré 23 ('43). But Béraldi Rel. II, p. 84, states that he was succeeded by his son-in-law, Pierre-Paul Gruel, in 1825. I have been unable to examine any binding bearing Deforge's signature before (at earliest) 1832. The firm of Deforge continued to appear in the Almanachs as late as 1849, though Gruel (misspelt *Grael*) appears in the 1832 Almanach. The Deforge problem is rendered still more complicated by a straight-grain morocco binding in my own collection on X. Saintine's Picciola,

1836, which might well be dated eight to ten years earlier, and a rocaille binding (on Beattie's *L'Ecosse* 1837) also in my own collection, which might well be dated 1842 or later.

DEGABRIEL, *Aîné*   *Paris*

Worked at St. Martin 261 from 1842–47.

DEGLE   *Paris*

Mentioned in the report of the 1823 Paris Exhibition as a binder of church books at rue du Roule 13. He received an honourable mention.

DEHAEN   *Lille*

The 1788–9 Lille Almanachs show a large family of this name, as follows:–

         DEHAENS, *Père* (or *L'Aîné*), 1788–89 and
             ,,   *Fils*, 1788, both at rue de l'Abbiette.
             ,,   *A.*, 1788–89, rue Mahieu–Mahieu.
             ,,   *André*, 1789, rue St. Maurice.
             ,,   *C. L.*, 1788–89, rue du Court-Debout.

DELABRE   *Lille*

Worked at Petite-Place 1788–89.

DELAERE   *Paris*

Recorded in the Almanachs at rue Jacob 23 from 1840–42.

DELAHAYE   *Paris*

Started at St. André-des-Arts 53 in 1821, and subsequently worked at Quai des Augustins 27 from 1832–43.

DELANAU   *Paris*

The only note of his appearance is at St. André-des-Arts 41 in 1815.

DELANIZEULLE, *François*   *Paris*

Thoinan, p. 241, notes him as working from 1779–90.

DELANNOY, *Aîné*   *Douai*

The Douai Almanach of 1788 cites his name at Grande Place.

DELANNOY *Paris*

According to the Paris Almanachs he worked at Marché-Neuf 9 from 1842–49.

DELANOE *Paris*

The 1840–43 Almanachs give his address as Hirondelle 18. It is not clear if he were identical with any of the three Delanoë working in 1847 listed below.

DELANOE *Paris*

Worked at Grès 10 in 1847 and may well be the same as the binder who appears in 1849 at Odéon 33.

DELANOE *Paris*

Appears between 1847 and 1849 at rue Voltaire 12.

DELANOE *Paris*

Noticed at Battoir St. André 4 in 1847. He may be the same as Delanoë, Père (see Brit. Mus. C. 63. b. 40), especially as there was a Delanoë, **Fils**, at the same address in 1849.

DELAPLACE *Paris*

First appears at Parcheminerie 19 in 1826 and finally at No. 2 in the same street in 1832.

DELATRE, Noel-Pierre-Louis (and Stationer) *Paris*

See Gruel II, p. 55. Worked from his reception in 1769 till at least 1789. His addresses seem to have been rue St. Jacques and rue Ste. Anne, butte St. Roch.

DELATTE *Paris*

Worked at rue de Carmes from 1797–1821, at the following numbers: 18 ('97); 17 ('03); 23 ('09).

DELAUNAY *Paris*

First noted in 1826 at Coq St. Honoré 8; then in 1838 at Pelican 7 and St. Dominique 38; and finally at Dragon 14 in 1843. Stated to have been a friend of Thouvenin.

DELAUNAY   *Paris*

Mentioned by Lesné ('27), p. 242. Stated to be a pupil of Herou, and to have started on his own about 1815 as a maker of book-binders' tools.

DELAUNAY, *Jeune*   *Paris*

Appears at Tracy 3 in 1847.

DELCOUR   *Bordeaux*

At rue des Trois-Conils ('33); Impasse de la Vieille-Monnaie ('36); rue des Trois-Conils ('39).

DELECROIX   *Lille*

At rue de Paris 261 from 1840–47.

DELENDON   *Paris*

Lesné ('27), p. 214, mentions him as an excellent gilder, but he does not appear in any of the Almanachs, possibly because, unlike many of his contemporaries, he never attempted to style himself "binder and gilder".

DELASALLE   *Lille*

At rue des Chats-Bossus 18 in 1836–42. His widow took over in 1843 and was still active in 1848.

DELETANG   *Paris*

Started at Pepinière 21 in 1838, and then worked at No. 35 bis from 1840–42.

DELETTANS   *Dunkirk*

Appears in the 1788 Almanach at Place Royale.

DELFIEU   *Paris*

Praised by Lesné ('27), p. 198, for the thinness and the evenness of his leather.

66

DELFORTRY and *CUISINIER*   *Lille*

>   At rue de Paris 1836–41. In 1842 Cuisinier (*q.v.*) set up on his own and Delfortry carried on at the same address till 1848, when he moved to rue de Béthune 26.

DELHALLE   *Paris*

>   The only mention which I have been able to trace is at Petites Ecuries 39 in 1843, but I have a nice half-morocco binding by him on an Arab MS.

DELIEGE, Père   *Amiens*

>   At Petite rue de Beauvais in 1826.

DELIEGE-BOIBERGE   *Amiens*

>   His address in 1826 was rue des Trois-Cailloux.

DELOMENIE   *Limoges*

>   In 1836 he was at rue de la Loi.

DELONG   *Toulouse*

>   At rue St. Pierre between 1833–38.

DELORME, René-Pierre   *Paris*

>   Thoinan, pp. 244 and 245, gives a long account of this binder (and print-dealer), received in 1774, and living at rue St. Jacques. He died at Montreuil, near Paris, on 8th April 1797. It seems unlikely that he is the same Delorme on whom Lesné ('27), pp. 41 and 140, made a slashing attack. Thoinan suggests that the latter may be Jean Delorme, who bound almanachs, etc.

ELORME   *Orleans*

>   At rue de la Préfecture in 1846.

ELOUVIER   *Paris*

>   Thoinan, p. 271, says that he was a son-in-law of J. B. Duplanil 1er and a master-binder.

DELPON   *Toulouse*

At rue des Gestes 9 in 1847–48.

DELSART, *Joachim*   *Lille*

Worked between 1829–38 at Marché des Fleurs 19.

DELSART, *Charles*   *Lille*

Succeeded the above (Joachim) at the same address in 1839 and continued till 1847.

DELUME   *Paris*

Cited in the Almanachs between 1826–32 at Harpe 13.

DEMAISON, P.

Worked about 1807. An illustration of his work appears in Desc. No. 457. It is typical of its date, and resembles the contemporary work of Simier, Thouvenin, Doll, Chilliat, etc.

DEMARANS

No details available.

DENAIX

No details available

DENAN, *Fils*   *Bordeaux*

Chemin du Sablonat ('36); rue Laville 2 ('48).

DENIS   *Angers*

At rue St. Laud in 1848.

DENY, *Etienne (and bookseller)*   *Metz*

Born at Metz and established first at rue de l'Evêché and then at rue de la Tête d'Or. Died September 22, 1860.

DEPOORTER, J.

This binder, possibly a Belgian, may have worked between 1815 and 1838. A fine example of his work in a heavy, ornate style, is illustrated in Sch. IV, 69.

DEROME   *Paris*

There were very many binders of this name, both before and during
our period. The latter are almost impossible to disentangle. A brief
note can be found on them in Thoinan, p.256.

DERUELLES   *Lille*

Worked at rue de la Barre 9 between 1833–40.

DESCORDES   *Paris*

Mentioned in the 1803 Almanach at rue d'Ecosse 4.

DESCORDES   *Paris*

Worked at Amandiers 7 between 1798–1803.

DESCORDES, *Aîné*   *Paris*

Cited from 1826–35 at Amandiers 15. Gruel tells me that a Desbordes,
Aîné was active in 1822; no doubt the same.

DESCORDES, *Jeune*   *Paris*

This binder and gilder first appears in 1826 at St. Jean-de-Beauvais 19.
From 1832–35 he was at Bucherie 9 and in the latter year is styled
"Fils" instead of "Jeune".

DESGRANGES-CHAMBELLAN   *Paris*

Appears in 1843 at Bouloi 1.

DESJARDINS   *Paris*

Worked at Harpe 58 from 1847–49.

DESLOGE

Another binder who is only known by name.

DESMAIS

His signature appears on a contemporary full red morocco binding,
with ornamentation in gilt of a typical kind on Legouvé's *Mérite des
Femmes*, 1813, in my own collection.

DESMAISONS   *Paris*

Appears in the 1821 Almanach at Sorbonne 2, but may have worked as early as 1814.

DESMARETS   *Paris*

Noted as at St. Jacques 110 in 1842.

DESPIERRES-LALANDE   *Paris*

They worked at Copeau 31 in 1838, and at No. 5 from 1840–43. Despierres later became binder to Napoleon III.

DESPILLY   *Paris*

According to Thoinan, p. 229, he succeeded in 1784 Louis-Balthazar de la Chavardière, one of the four stationers, mapmakers, and binders attached to the Court. Later he was styled "Stationer of the Emperor", but may, like his predecessor, have also done bookbinding. For an example of his alleged binding see Pl. 2658/1 of Olivier's Manuel.

DESSAUX   *Paris*

Worked at Hautefeuille 20 from 1840–43.

DESENNE   *Paris*

First noted at Plâtre St. Jacques in 1838, and later at St. Jacques 71 in 1847.

DEVAINE   *Paris*

In 1843 he was established at Oratoire 12, and four years later at rue Neuve des Petits-Champs 50.

DEVAUX, Edmé   *Dijon*

Did cheap binding for the Dijon Library between 1823–37. His address was 20 rue de l'Ecole de Droit.

DEVERS, André   *Lyons*

There were two binders of the name, both André. In 1810 one was at rue de l'Hospice 32 and the other at rue de Bourbon 84. In 1813 and 1816 they were at rue de l'Hôpital (formerly de l'Hospice) 54 and rue d'Egypte 4. In 1821–32 the Indicateur shows one at rue de l'Hôpital 54. I have a 3-volume Demoustier dated 1809, bound in blond calf which would seem attributable to one of the above.

DEVERS, *Claude* *Paris and Lyons*

According to the Paris Almanachs he worked at Galande 61 from 1826–49. His work, or his relatives' work, is illustrated in Sch. 97/100, Bér. V, 15, and Maggs' 70th Birthday Catalogue 223.

DEVERS, *Joseph* *Lyons*

At Monnaie 1 in 1842.

DEVERS, *Pierre* *Lyons*

Started in 1821 at Savoie 10, and from 1832–42 worked at Grande rue Mercière 44.

DEVERS, *Pierre-François* *Lyons*

Worked from 1813–42, all at Place des Célestins 7, except for the last year, when he moved to Ambroise 14.

DEVERS-MAILLY, *Joseph* *Lyons*

Started in 1810 at Grande rue Mercière 25, then in 1813 at Palais-Grillet 6, and from 1832–42 at Monnaie 6.

DEVILLE, *Mlle.* *Paris*

Worked at Sorbonne 12 from 1815–16. She is described as a "sewer and gatherer" and was probably not a "binder".

DEVILLERS *Paris*

Figures in the 1836–49 Almanachs at Augustin 55, but may have started as early as 1825.

DEWATINES (& LEROY) *Lille*

He worked between 1838 and 1848 at Terrasse Ste. Catherine 8, for the first year with Leroy and then alone. Specimens of his work of later date are to be found in Desc. II, 212 and 238, and also in Bér. V, 280.

DHERCLONVILLE, *Georges (and bookseller)* *Metz*

Born at Metz March 2, 1729. Set up at rue de la Tête d'Or in 1764. Died at rue du Petit-Paris January 31, 1805.

DHERCLONVILLE, *Augustin* *Metz*

Son of above, born in 1768, was a binder only and died June 30, 1844.

DIETRICH

Working about the last decade of the eighteenth century (see Sch. II, 159).

DIGOT

Only his name has been noted as inside our period.

DION *Lille*

At rue Esquermoise 13 from 1845–48.

DOIGNIES *Paris*

Active from 1815–49 at the following addresses: Carmes 34 ('15); 24 ('26); 23 ('36).

DOLL, F. *Paris*

This binder is often described as the Emperor's favourite binder, though I have not been able to trace any foundation for such a description.

He probably started work about 1796–98, and his early ticket gives his address as rue de Seine 38. The 1809 Almanach shows that he had then transferred to No. 53. In 1815 he was at Mazarine 16 (see label on Sch. III, 214) and by 1821 at Marais St. Germain 13.

Nothing seems to be known of Doll's apprenticeship, if any, but it would perhaps be fair to assume that he started in the workshop of the younger Bozérian who, whatever his own merits or demerits as a binder, seems to have provided an excellent nursery from which came binders like Thouvenin and Lefèbvre.

Maggs' Cat. 661, Nos. 3, 70, 141, 160, and 198, and Sch. III, 209/214 give excellent illustrations of Doll's three principal styles: (1) the transition style represented primarily by the work of the two Bozérians

72

and by much of the early work of Lefèbvre, Chilliat, Thouvenin, Simier, etc. My own specimen of Doll's binding, on Grandmaison's *Amours* ('04) is typical of this style; (2) Doll's calf bindings with classical motives approximating to the combined work of Bozérian and Lefèbvre, and to some of Mairet's bindings; and (3) typical Restoration bindings of the 1815-25 period (see Maggs 661/70). Occasionally, as in Sch. III, 209, he produced a binding which appears to be a pure imitation of English work of the same period.

The presence of the crowned cypher of Queen Marie-Amélie on the Doll binding, Maggs 661/198, unless added later, would appear to show that Doll was still working after 1830.

DOLLOT   *Dôle*

I owe his name to a French provincial librarian.

DONDEY-DUPRE   *Paris*

Sch. III, 269, shows an excellent binding on a work dated 1814 with which it is obviously contemporary. The label states that it was bound by D.-D., stationer, of rue Neuve St.-Marc 10.

DORIN, *Antoine*   *Lyons*

Given in the 1810 Lyons *Indicateur* as working at Thomassin 14.

DORINAL   *Bordeaux*

At rue du Loup ('33-'36); rue Gouvion ('39).

DORIS   *Paris*

Appears in the 1799 Almanach Typographique at Cimetière-St. André-des-Arts and then in the ('09) Almanach at rue d'Ecosse 3.

DORLEANS   *Paris*

Worked at Impasse St. Claude, Montmartre, from 1842-49.

DORMAEL   *Lille*

At rue de l'Abbaye de Loos 37 ('29); then at rue J. J. Rousseau 35/37. ('43/'42). His widow continued between 1843-48.

DORY   *Paris*

Listed as a gilder as well as a binder, at Carmes 12 in 1797; St. Jean-de-Beauvais 22 in 1815 and No. 24 in 1821.

DRAGONNE   *Paris*

Both binder and gilder, he worked at rue St. Honoré 24 from 1816–26. The only specimen of his work I know is that described and illustrated in the E. Brouwet Sale Catalogue of November 13, 1834, No. 92, where one of his bindings is described and illustrated. It is very much in the English style. The tooling round the sides is of the rather heavy type used by Charles Lewis, and was no doubt founded on the heavy English tools which Hering imported from his English relations.

DRANNER   *Strassburg*

The only specimen of this binder known to me occurs in Desc. II, 271, and dates about 1820–25, of which period's strapping effects it is a good specimen.

DRAPIER   *Lille*

Quoted in the 1788 Lille Almanach as at rue de Courtrai.

DREYSPRING, *Chrétien*   *Strassburg*

At Grande rue de la Grange 25 in 1824.

DRIAN   *Lyons*

Worked at Paradis 2 in 1832.

DRUART   *Lille*

At rue des Trois Mollettes 42 ('36); rue Doudin 6 ('45); rue Esquermoise 84 ('46–'48).

DUBERNET   *Bordeaux*

In 1848 was at rue des Trois-Conils ('37).

DUBOIS   *Paris*

The 1797–1803 Almanachs give his address as Liberté 85.

DUBOIS, *Marin*   *Paris*

Thoinan, p. 264, states that he was received in 1777, and resided at rue Amandier 17 till about 1804. The latter is confirmed by the 1803 Almanach.

DUBOIS   *Paris*

Worked between 1821 and 1842 in rue d'Argenteuil at various addresses as follows: 36 ('21); 47 ('26); 52 ('35).

DUBOIS   *Toulouse*

At rue Royale in 1807.

DUBOIS   *Paris*

The 1847 Almanach records him at Boulevard du Temple 33.

DUBOIS, *Aîné*   *Boulogne*

The Boulogne Annuary for 1841–42 refers to him as a binder and stationer working at Simoneau 2.

DUBOIS-CANON   *Angers*

At rue St. Laud between 1831–40.

DUBOIS-CUCHEVAL   *Boulogne*

Also binder and stationer from 1841–42. Addresses: Siblequin 25 and later Passage d'Herlen 27.

DUBOS, *Frères*   *Paris*

According to the 1847 Almanach resided at Ste. Marguérite 18.

DUBOS, *Veuve et Fils*   *Paris*

Worked at Ste. Marguérite 18 from 1838–42.

DUBOSQ   *Paris*

First active at Sept Voies 3 in 1803; transferred to St. Jacques 110 in 1809, where he was still active in 1821.

75

DUBOSQ, *Fils*   *Paris*

First reported at Ecosse 2 in 1809, and last in 1826 at St. Jacques 110, where his father had previously practised.

DUBRAY   *Paris*

At St. Martin 199 in 1847.

DUBUC   *Paris*

The 1847 Almanach places him at Harpe 46.

DUCASTIN, *Alexis-Jacques*   *Paris*

This descendant of a long line of binders was received in 1778 and, according to Thoinan, was living in 1787 at Mont-St. Hilaire. He married a daughter of Jean Baptiste Ier Duplanil.

DUCASTIN, *Père*   *Paris*

He may be the same as, or a son of, Alexis-Jacques. No Ducastin appears in the 1797 Almanach, but when such a name appears in the 1803 Almanach, it is at Mont-St. Hilaire, 5–6, i.e. the same street as Alexis-Jacques in 1787. Whoever he may have been, Ducastin (Père) worked till 1826, having moved about 1821 to St. Jacques 118. My own collection contains a calf binding by Ducastin (almost certainly the "père") on Legouvé's *Mérite des Dames* n.d. It does not appear from its present poorish condition to have ever been of the first class. There is an illustration of his work in Rahir Cat., Vol. VI, No. 2078.

DUCASTIN, *Fils*   *Paris*

He is first noted in the 1821 Almanach at St. Jacques 103, and later in 1832 at St. Jean-de-Beauvais 18, where he appears to have worked till at least 1847. Thoinan, p. 268, also refers to his having been at some time at rue de Savoie. He apparently dropped the "Fils" about 1838. Both he and his father appear to have signed just as Ducastin, and their respective work is therefore hard to distinguish.

DUCHEMIN   *Angers*

At rue Baudrière between 1831–48.

DUCHON   *Paris*

Lesné ('27), p. 377, refers to him as one of the leading marblers of end papers and edges, a work seldom done by the binder himself.

DUCROCQ   *Paris*

The only date which I have been able to attach to this binder is 1842, in the Almanach for which year his address is given as Maçons 3. A binding by him is described in Boerner, Cat. XXI, No. 187.

DUCROS   *Paris*

Worked at Montagne Ste. Geneviève 37 in 1840.

DUFET   *Paris*

At Passage Dauphine in 1847.

DUFEY, Fils   *Nancy*

Thoinan, p. 269, quotes him as working in 1791, and from a binding on **Falconer's** *Shipwreck* dated 1817 he was certainly working at that date. I have also a good example of his work in a semi-Jansenist dark blue morocco binding on the 1667 edition (Elzevier) of *Prudentius*, signed at the foot of the spine.

DUFEY-BOULON   *Lille*

Rue de la Monnaie ('29); rue des Trois Mollettes 30 ('30).

DUFEY-LEPERRE   *Lille*

Rue Coqueret ('29); rue Dondin 19 ('30–'39).

DUGAY   *Agen*

See B. de F. 2316. Worked about 1840.

DUJARDIN, Victor   *Paris*

Noted as at rue Basse du Rempart 62 in 1842, and at Joubert 47 from 1847 onwards.

DUMERGUE   *Paris*

At Hanover 8 from 1843–49.

DUMONT   *Paris*

The 1838 Almanach mentions him at St. Jean-de-Beauvais 15.

DUMONT, *L. J.*

See Bér. Cat. III, 307, where he is given as binding *Six Romances by Charles Lis.*

DUMONT-GRARE   *Abbeville*

Worked at Marché du Fromage 8 in 1826.

DUPERRON   *Toulouse*

At rue des Chartreux in 1807.

DUPIN, *Antoine*   *Lyons*

The 1821 **Indicateur** gives his address as Place Confort 17.

DUPIN, *J. F.*   *Lyons*

Noted as at Place Confort 17 from 1810–16. Probably the father, or at least a relation of Antoine (*q.v.*).

DUPIN, *Fils*   *Lyons*

Sch. III, 273, illustrates an excellent binding by "Dupin fils à Lyon" on an 1817 *Heures*, while my own collection contains an extraordinary binding on the 1814 edition of Lafontaine's *Contes* (Lefèvre), with green morocco spine, with red inlays, and tortoiseshell lacquered sides apparently on thin metal. There is nothing to show if the binder is or is not the same as Antoine or J.F. (*q.v.*).

DUPLANIL   *Paris*

The members of this distinguished family of binders, who were active during the 1789–1848 period are by no means easy to identify. The first two members of the family, Jean and Jean-Baptiste 1er had, as it is clear from Thoinan, p.270, died before 1789, and we have therefore to try and deal with the three sons of the latter, i.e. Jean-Baptiste II, Pierre, and Nicolas; also with Duplanil "Père" and "Fils" of the Restoration-Louis Philippe period, and with a certain Duplanil "Veuve".

DUPLANIL, *Jean-Baptiste II*   *Paris*

Received in 1759, lived at rue Judas in 1779, and may be the same as
the Duplanil in the 1803 Almanach at Judas 13.

DUPLANIL, *Fils*   *Paris*

He figures in the Almanachs from 1821–36 (he may have started rather
earlier, as Bér. Rel. I, p. 34, mentions a Duplanil at 29 rue des Sept-
Voies in 1814). His addresses were: St. Jacques 103 ('21); Savoie 6
('24); Grenelle 59 and Bac 75 ('35). Gruel ('05), II, p. 74, states that
he exhibited as late as 1844. He received a silver medal in 1834.
He styles himself as binder to Madame Royale (daughter of Louis XVI
and Marie-Antoinette), who became, by marriage to the son of
Charles X, H.R.H. la Duchesse d'Angoulême, and later, in 1824,
"la Dauphine".
His official bindings, as illustrated in Sch. III, 275–80, are easily
recognisable, and can even be dated with some accuracy. A binding
in my own collection in full morocco, signed at foot of spine
"Duplanil", on the *Vie de Mme. Louise*, 2 vol., 1823, can also be
reasonably identified as his work, since it bears a stamp with the
Duchesse's arms and the address of Chateau de Villeneuve-l'Etang.
This is perhaps the occasion to refer to the identification (far less
easy) of the work of other members of the family. I have been unable
to identify any specimens of pre-1800 work by the three sons of
Jean-Baptiste 1er. The task of separating the work of the two
Duplanils working after 1815, where not specially indicated, as in
the case of many of the bindings of Duplanil Fils, is far from easy.
An examination of the four items illustrated in Desc. II provides a
good exercise. My own guess would be Nos. 82 and 372 for the
father, and Nos. 314 and 355 for the son.
Duplanil, Fils, married the daughter of Ottmann I, whence the
firm of Ottmann-Duplanil (*q.v.*).

DUPLANIL, *Veuve*   *Paris*

Her address in the 1803 Almanach was Sept-Voies 6. My guess would
be that she was the widow of Pierre, and the mother of "Père".

DUPLANIL, *Nicolas*   *Paris*

Received in 1772, and lived in 1779 at rue d'Ecosse. He may be the
same as the binder of which a passing mention appears in the 1797
Almanach at Cul-de-Sac des Bœufs 2.

79

DUPLANIL, Pierre (? and "Père")   *Paris*

Received in 1768, and stated by Thoinan to have lived at rue des Sept Voies. From 1809–32 the Almanachs give a Duplanil as working at Sept Voies, and from 1821 this Duplanil entitles himself "Père". It seems difficult to believe that only one Duplanil can have been working in the same street for sixty-four years, and it may therefore be reasonable to suppose that the period 1768–1832 is covered by two generations at least.

DUPONT, Michel   *Lyons*

According to Gruel I, p. 148, he lived at rue Tupin and was executed in 1793.

DUPRE   *? Paris*

Gruel (July 18, 1849) tells me that he succeeded Andrieu in 1844.

DUPUIDS   *Paris*

The 1836 Almanach gives his address as Observance 5. He moved two years later to No. 1, where he was working in 1847.

DUPUIS, Mme.   *Paris*

Appears in the 1836 Almanach at Foin-St. Germain 17.

DUQUESNE, Desiré   *Lille*

At Place de la Mairie 27 between 1829–48.

DURAND   *Paris*

Worked at Amandiers 20 in 1797 and at No. 18 in 1803; No. 17 ('09–'15). May be the binder of Sch. III, 240. (See also Rousseau-Girard 1950 Cat. 13/No. 5824.)

DURAND   *Dijon*

The Librarian of the Dijon Library, who delighted in encouraging local talent, in 1823 gave him to bind an in-folio edition of Voltaire's *Henriade*, presented by the Comte d'Artois. Durand kept it for four years, and the Librarian had to appeal to the Mayor to secure its return, when its binding was eventually finished by Pralon. The Librarian, in writing to the Mayor, states that Durand, then living at 7 rue Tonnellerie, had changed his residence five times since 1823 had left his wife and was neglecting his work, and that the speedy recovery of the volume was therefore desirable.

DURAND, *Adolphe*

R.L.B. reports him as active from 1832–64.

DURAND, *Alphonse*   *Paris*

The 1832–36 Almanachs give his address as St. Jacques 229.

DURAND, *Antoine*   *Paris*

Received 1765, and according to Thoinan, p. 272, still working under the Convention. His address in 1782 was Mont-St. Hilaire. He is probably the binder with ticket at Carmes 1, see Sch. III, 239. I have a 2-vol. La Fontaine's *Contes*, published 1795, in a similar binding and with the same ticket, which omits any mention of "Antoine".

DURAND, *Fils*   *Paris*

Worked consistently at Amandiers 17 from 1826–49.

DURAULT   *Paris*

The Almanach Typographique mentions him at rue des Amandiers in 1799.

DURRE   *Bordeaux*

Worked at Place St. Germain 12 ('36–'39) and rue Huguerie 4 ('48).

DURRE, *A.*   *Bordeaux*

At rue St. James 57 in 1848.

DURU, *Hippolite*   *Paris*

Worked on his own 1843–46.

DURVILLE   *Montpellier*

Binder to the Musée Fabre. Exhibited at the Montpellier Exhibition in November 1839, when his address was rue du Palais 9. Later he worked at rue Embouque d'Or.

DUTERTRE   *Boulogne*

Noted in the 1840–41 Year Book as a binder and stationer at Siblequin 68.

DUTERTRE   *Marseilles*

At Quai du Port between 1812 and 1815.

DUTERTRE   *Nantes*

Addresses: Basse Grande-rue ('04); au Pilori ('08); rue de Briord ('17).

DUTHERLIN   *Paris*

Appears in the Almanachs as follows: St. Jacques 240 (1797); St. Jean-de-Beauvais 6 (1803).

DUTITRE

Nicolas Rauch Cat. 1/1948 Nos. 299/30 shows him as a rocaille binder of the Bonfils type, date about 1843.

DUTREUIL, Joseph   *Limoges*

Master-binder 1764–89.

DUVAL   *Nantes*

At Place du Commerce in 1817.

DUVAL, Pierre   *Lyons*

Given by the 1810 Indicateur as working at Hospice 52.

ECHAUBARD   *Rouen*

Alas only a name.

EDET, Jeune   *Rouen*

I have seen his label at rue Beauvaisine 7, près de la Crosse, but cannot be sure if he was a binder.

ENGEL, Charles-Théophile   *Strassburg*

At Petites Boucheries 108 in 1824.

ENGEL   *Paris*

According to Bér. Rel. II, p. 54, he was born in Würtemburg in 1811, served as an apprentice in Tubingen and Dijon, and later in Paris with Wagner and Kleinhans. He possibly set up on his own in 1838 at Pont-du-Lodi 3. For his future career see *Engel-Schaeck*.

ENGEL-SCHAECK   *Paris*

These two brothers-in-law founded a mechanical bindery in 1838. From 1847 they were domiciled at Suger 20.

ENGRAND   *Paris*

Lesné ('27), p. 123, speaks of him as an excellent producer of the plainer type of end-paper.

ENGUEHARD, *Léon*   *Lyons*

The 1810 Lyons Indicateur mentions him as at Grand' rue Mercière, maison Orsel-Deschamps 1.

ENSFELDER, *Ch.*   *Strassburg*

At Hallebardes 8 in 1846.

ENTOIR

No details have come to hand.

ESCARAGUEL   *Paris*

Worked at Amandiers 15 from 1809–38, and from then till 1842 at Fouare 15. I have never seen a specimen of his work, though he figures consistently in the Almanachs for thirty-three years. The Scaraguel in the Almanach Typographique 1799 is no doubt the same.

ESNAULT   *Paris*

See *Lard-Esnault*. A label on a work in the B.M. by Isouard dedicated to the Duke of Sussex shows a stationer named Esnault working at 92 rue de Richelieu about 1811.

ESTEYVE, *Jean-Baptiste*   *Limoges*

Master-binder in 1789.

ETARD

The only specimen of his work known to me is illustrated in Sch. III, No. 310. I have seen it and it is rather rough work, in the Bonfils style, and perhaps a little later than the date of the book (1828).

EVEND *Paris*

Appears in the 1847–49 Almanachs at rue Petite du Bac 12.

EVEUS *Paris*

A binder and gilder, mentioned in 1843 at Ste. Placide 1.

EYRARD *Paris*

Worked at St. Jacques 22 from 1816–35. I saw in December 1949 a binding by A. Evrard in the shop of M-R Gonot, of Paris.

FAGE *Paris*

Appears at Meslay 34 in 1815.

FAILLE *Rheims*

D. d'E. states that he exhibited in 1849; he may therefore have been already working before 1848.

FALHOU & Cie. *Paris*

This firm, residing at Quai des Augustins 15 in 1821, describe themselves as edge-gilders.

FALKEMBERG *Boulogne*

The Boulogne Year Books for 1839–47 give his address as Carreaux 6.

FARGE, *Bernard* *Lyons*

According to Gruel I, p. 148, he lived at rue de la Grenette, and was executed in 1793.

FARJAT *Paris*

The 1842–49 Almanachs give his addresses as Chabrol 28 and Ménilmontant 7.

FASSIOT, Antoine *Lyons*

At Thomassin 8 in 1842, according to the Lyons Indicateur.

FAUCHET, P. *Paris*

No doubt the same as the *Fauché* of whom Lesné ('27) speaks well on p. 306. He had a long career, first at Monsieur le Prince 19 in 1821, then at Mathurin 11 in 1826, and finally at Harpe 66 from 1835–49. Illustrations of his work are to be found in Sch. III, 303, and Maggs 661/168.

FAUQUEUX

I only know his name as a binder of the period.

FAURE *Paris*

At Petit-Bourbon 9 and Garancière 1 in 1842, and at Harpe 18 in 1849.

FAYOLLE, Anthelme *Lyons*

According to the Lyons Indicateur, was first at Raisin 33 in 1810, and then at No. 7 from 1813–32.

FAYOLLE, Jean-Marie *Lyons*

Noted at Raisin 7 in 1842.

FELIX *Paris*

According to the Almanachs he worked at Sorbonne 6 from 1832; at Mathurin 14 from 1836; and at Harpe 85 from 1847. An example of his work is described in Desc. II, 295.

FELIX, Veuve *Paris*

Was at Francs-Bourgeois 11 in 1842.

FERIN, Mesdames *? Lyons*

This signature figures on an undated polyglot *Horace* in my own collection, bound apparently about 1845–50.

FERRIER *Paris*

Recorded at Pot-de-Fer 5 in 1842 and at Vaugirard 57 bis in 1847.

FETIL   *Paris*

    Appears in the 1797–1803 Almanachs at rue d'Ecosse 3.

FETIL   *Paris*

    Mentioned by Thoinan, p. 285, as a stationer, mapmaker, and binder; living at "Entrée du Faubourg St. Denis" about 1800.

FETIL   *Paris*

    Mentioned by Lesné as a skilful edge-gilder about 1820.

FEUTRAY

    No details are known to me.

FISCHBACK, H.   *Strassburg*

    At Grand'rue 152 in 1846.

FIXON (*See* LEON-FIXON)   *Paris*

FIXON (*See* FRANCOISE CALLIER *née* FIXON)

FLANNEAU, J.   *Paris*

    First appears in 1840 at St.-Sauveur 33 and 30 [*sic*] and then in 1843 at Petit-Carême 2.

FLICHE   *Paris*

    At Cannettes 20 in 1840 and then at Cherche-Midi 33 from 1842–49.

FOCK, F.   *Paris*

    Rue Mazarine 28 from 1847–49.

FONTAINE   *Angers*

    Worked at rue St. Laud in 1831.

FORCY

    D. d'E. quotes him, somewhat doubtfully, as working in 1822.

FOREST   *Paris*

   Recorded in the Almanachs from 1826–47, in which year the firm
   was styled as Forest Frères. The addresses were: rue Neuve des
   Mathurins 13 ('26); 38 ('32); 54 ('42).

FOREST   *Paris*

   At rue Petit-Crucifix in 1843; and at rue Neuve des Mathurins 67
   in 1847.

FOUBERT, L.-A.   *Paris*

   Worked at Bibliothèque 16 in 1842.

FOUCOU   *Marseilles*

   Makes a solitary appearance in 1819 at rue d'Aubagne.

FOUGERAY   *Paris*

   Founded in 1842 at Pont-aux-Choux 17 and then from 1843–49 at No. 7.

FOUQUART   *Douai*

   The 1788 Douai Almanach mentions him at rue des Wetz.

FOUQUART   *Douai*

   Another binder of the same name, also working in 1788, but at rue
   des Ecoles.

FOURE (*or FOURRE, Aîné*)   *Paris*

   Worked at Mont-St. Hilaire 11 from 1797–1803.

FOURE, *Jeune*   *Paris*

   Makes his only appearances at St. Jean-de-Beauvais in 1799 and at
   rue de Carmes in 1803.

FOURE, *Jeune*   *Paris*

   His addresses were: St. Jean-de-Beauvais 20 ('21); Montagne 54 ('26);
   Carmes 26 ('32); St. Séverin 14 ('38). Lesné ('27), pp. 128, 350, and
   354; treats his work at length. He evidently tries to be fair, but hates
   his overfast work, and his superficiality, and cannot resist quoting
   his nickname "le rôtisseur" which we should translate "the scorcher".
   I have not seen any samples of his work.

87

FOURNET, A.

A somewhat provincial work by this binder connected with Marshal Lannes is illustrated in Sch. III, 221.

FOURNIER   *Limoges*

Quoted by D. d'E. as working in 1817.

FOURNIER   *Limoges*

Worked at rue du Temple between 1836–48.

FOURNIER   *Limoges*

In 1846–48 was working at rue du Consulat.

FRABULY

His name appears in the Firmin-Didot Cat. ('83), 137.

FRANCE   *Paris*

At rue Galande in 1799 and at Noyers 3 in 1803.

FRANCOIS, *Louis-Joseph*   *Paris*

Thoinan refers to him on p. 287 as received in 1776, and residing at Mont-St. Hilaire. He must have been active at least till 1794, the date of publication of a work illustrated in Sch. II, No. 186, and signed by him.

FREMONT

Mentioned in Gruel ('05), p. 83, but without any indication of date.

FRERE   *Paris*

Appears at Ecosse 4 in 1803.

FREY, *Th.*   *Strassburg*

At Grand'rue 161 in 1846.

FRICHET, *Veuve*   *Paris*

Showed commercial bindings in the 1834 Paris Exhibition.

FRICK, J.

? Outside period. See Album in my own collection and Maggs 661/264.

FRISE, *Comtesse de*

I have been unable to trace any details.

FRUCHET   *Paris*

In 1816 at Guénégaud 1, and then in 1821 at Monsieur-le-Prince 19.

FURRET   *Nantes*

At rue La Fayette 1 in 1848.

GALETTE   *Paris*

Worked at Mazarine 47 from 1842–49.

GALLARD   *Nantes*

At rue de la Commune in 1831.

GAMET   *Paris*

According to the 1803 Almanach he was working at rue d'Ecosse 7, and Thoinan, p. 290, tends to show that he had been located there for some time.

GANDY (*or GANDIT*)   *Lyons*

First appears at Paradis 2 in 1832, and then at Ferrandière 11 ten years later.

GANON

Worked about 1824.

GARIN   *Paris*

A restorer, mentioned at Seine 51 in the 1840 Almanach.

GARNIER   *Paris*

At rue Charpentier 4 in 1840 and at rue Pontoise 21 in 1849.

GAROS, *Don*

Lesné ('27), p. 307, treats him in such disparaging terms that it seems probable that he is not a real binder, but that he could be recognised at the time by Lesné's readers.

GARRIGUES   *Toulouse*

At rue des Gestes ('47) and rue Boulbonne ('48).

GASTINEAU   *Angers*

At rue Baudrière in 1848.

GAUBAL

D. d'E. quotes a binding on an 1828 work in the Backer Cat. No. 2600.

GAUDARD, *Etienne*   *Dijon*

Born at Dôle in 1792. He first established himself at Dijon in 1819 at rue de Griffon 21, and later his labels show that he worked at Portel 5. He does not appear to have worked for the Dijon Library till about 1830. He may have started work at Dôle before 1819, and the contemporary *Lyons* Indicateurs seem to show that the same E. Gaudard may have also worked in Lyons at rue St. Jacques 110. Gaudard evidently maintained close contact with Dôle, and his three children were born there, i.e. Celestine (1822), Eleanore ('23), and François ('26). Samples of his work are described and illustrated in Sch. 289 and Bér. V, 241. The Dijon Librarian reports his work as sober, but elegant in design, and of good workmanship. He exhibited at the Dijon Arts Exhibition in 1837.

GAUDELLE   *Paris*

Working at St. Jacques 134 in 1821.

GAUDIN   *Paris*

First found at Sorbonne 3 in 1839 and then from 1840–49 at Monsieur-le-Prince 22.

GAUDREAU   *Paris*

Thoinan, p. 298, says that he was working as early as 1798 at rue
de la Harpe. My own researches show him as at Harpe 251 from
1803–15, and from then till 1838 at St. Jacques 110. A 3-volume Boileau
dated 1813 in my own collection bears his label at the latter address.
A *Mérite des Femmes* dated 1824 has no label. My other binding by
Gaudreau (signed on spine) is on Delille's Printemps 1803, and may
be bound by this Gaudreau, or the one listed immediately below.
It is much earlier in style. Another specimen of this binder is
illustrated in Sch. II, 104.

GAUDREAU   *Paris*

Thoinan, p. 298, states that another Gaudreau was working 1798–1803
at Charretière (?), though I am only able to trace Dlle Gaudreau as
active in 1803.

GAUDREAU, *Dlle*   *Paris*

Working at Charretière 5 in 1803, and then at No. 9 in 1815.

GAUGAIN, H.   *Paris*

Seems to have changed his address constantly between 1797 and
1838, as follows: Carmes 15 ('97); Charretière 6 ('03); St. Jean-de-
Beauvais 11 ('15); Ecosse 8 ('26); St. Jacques 39 ('32); Charretière 9
('36).

GAUTHIER   *Paris*

At Richer 27 bis in 1847.

GAVOIS-GRARE   *Abbeville*

Noted in 1826 at rue de la Tartarie 2.

GEISLER   *Strassburg*

See Gruel ('05), II, p. 87. Was working about 1794.

GENDARME   *Paris*

Recorded in the 1821 Almanach as at Harpe 45.

GENDRE
Agen

Sch. III, **222**, illustrates a binding by him on a volume dated 1806, and which appears to be of about that date. In the curious label inside, which gives his prices, and his address as Pont-de-Garonne 44, he states that he has been established for fifteen years (i.e. approximately between 1791 and 1806).

GENET

This binder's name appears on a binding (*c.* 1830) in my own collection.

GENTIL, *le Jeune*
Paris

At Richelieu-Sorbonne 2 in 1809. The Almanach Typographique 1799 gives a Gentil*l*, Jeune, at Sept-Voies, who may be the same.

GENTY
Paris

His address in 1803 was Cluny (?).

GEOFFROY
Paris

In 1842 at Neuve St. Martin 30, and in 1843 at Grand Hurleur 2.

GEORGES .
Angers

At rue du Ralliement in 1831 and at rue de l'Oisellerie ('40–'48).

GEORGES, D.
Marseilles

Started at rue 1er Calade 12 in 1841; moved to No. 4 in ('44); and back to No. 12 in 1846.

GERMAIN, *Leonard*
Limoges

A master-binder in 1789, and possibly active from 1742 or ('56).

GERMAIN-SIMIER
Paris

Appears in the 1832–49 Almanachs, but may have worked on his own earlier. Addresses: Bons Enfans 34 ('32); Pagevin 2 ('35); St. Honoré 357 ('36); Croix des Petits-Champs 19 ('40); St. Honoré 245 ('47). Possibly a son-in-law of the younger Simier. In my own collection there is a pleasing calf binding of his on Gilbert's *Œuvres* ('23). Specimens of his work are also illustrated in Desc. II, 98 and Rahir VI, 2027.

GERMAIN, *Jean-Baptiste*   *Limoges*

Master-binder 1766–89. Chosen to represent the Binders' Corporation at the Tiers-Etat de Limoges in February 1789.

GEUGNOT   *Paris*

The 1840–47 Almanachs locate him at Godot 24.

GEUGNOT   *Paris*

A second binder of this name appears in 1847–49 at Ville-l'Evêque 2 bis.

GEZEK, *Joseph*   *Alsace*

D. d'E. describes a masterpiece of binding ingenuity by him with Strassburg Cathedral stamped in small tools.

GIBERT   *Aix*

At rue du Collége in 1822.

GILET   *Paris*

Lesné ('27), p. 198, refers to the thinness and evenness of the skins supplied by Gilet and Delfieu. Though he admits their many advantages from the points of view of appearance, elasticity, and general "play", he finds that their extreme thinness makes them less solid than the best English skins. A Thouvenin binding in my own collection on the *Correspondence of Pope Clement* XIV dated 1827, tends to confirm the above remarks.

GILLON   *Lille*

The 1788–89 Almanach lists him at rue du Dragon.

GILLON, *Aîné*   *Paris*

At Mazarine 26 in 1847.

GINAIN   *Paris*

One of the greatest and most refined binders of his day, of whose history little authentic is known. His work approximates to that of the elder Thouvenin and, like him, he may be a product of the

93

Bozérian Jeune nursery. The Almanachs cite him from 1821–49, first and mainly at Argenteuil 23, and only in 1847 at St. Honoré 290. He seems to have attached his fortunes closely to Louis-Philippe, and after the latter's succession he became "Binder to the King", though it is not clear at what exact date. Many illustrations of his work can be found in such works as Desc. Cat. II, Maggs Cat. 661, Béraldi Cat., etc. One would like to know much more about him than we appear to do.

GIRARD   *Angers*

At rue des Tonneliers in 1848.

GIRARD   *Paris*

Active at Trois Frères 25 from 1840–49.

GIRARDET

An elaborate binding by him is described and illustrated in Sch. III, 283. There is no exact indication of its date, and none of his place of working. See also Bér. Rel. II, plate 61.

GIRARDET, D.   *Strassburg*

At Fosses-des-Tailleurs 13 in 1846.

GIRARDOT

My own collection contains a specimen by this binder, on Bourasse's Cathédrales ('43). It is a plain half chagrin with blind stamped lines.

GIROUX, *Alphonse (et Cie.)*   *Paris*

He appears to have worked, as an individual or as a firm, approximately between 1826–48 at Coq St. Honoré 7. Though he signed his name at the foot of the spine of bindings and used a label similar to those used by binders, there seems no doubt that neither he nor his firm executed their own bindings. This is borne out by the fact that he is never listed in the Almanachs as a binder. He almost certainly commissioned bindings by the best executants of the day. My own collection contains an excellent specimen of his shop, executed for the Comte de Chambord, and others are illustrated in the Béraldi Cat. III and in Maggs 661, Nos. 227 and 261.

GLAISE, A. *Paris*

The 1832–36 Almanachs show him at Bucherie 1.

GOBOL *Lyons*

The Lyons Indicateur for 1842 gives his name at Pazzy 3.

GODARD *Abbeville*

Worked at rue des Minimes in 1826.

GODEFROY *Paris*

At Faubourg-Montmartre 4 from 1847–49.

GODEREAU *Paris*

Lesné ('27), pp. 215 and 306, refers to him as among the best class binders of his day, and as living in the Quartier St. Hilaire. I have not, however, been able to trace him in the Almanachs.

GODEREAU, *Femme* *Paris*

Figures in the 1797–98 Almanachs as at Charretière 6.

GOHIER-DESFONTAINES, *et Cie.* *Paris*

Gohier appears to have worked on his own in 1839 at Feydeau 28 and then as above at Boulevard Montmartre 1 in 1842–43.

GONNET *Paris*

Shown in the '42–'43 Almanachs at Maçons-Sorbonne 17.

GONNET, *Aîné* *Paris*

At Amandiers 15 from 1840–49.

GONNET, *Jeune* *Paris*

Noted at St. Jean-de-Beauvais 24 in 1842.

GORJUX *Marseilles*

At rue d'Aubagne 95 in 1847–48.

GOSSELIN, *Jean-Baptiste* *Paris*

This binder was "received" as early as 1767, and Thoinan, p. 308, gives quite a full account of his career. The post-Revolutionary Almanachs quote a Gosselin at different Nos. in rue St. Jacques up to as late as 1836. While it is difficult to believe that the original Jean-Baptiste had seventy years of active binding, we must, pending further information, assume that any other assumption would be non-proven.

The known addresses are as follows: First, St. Jacques ?; 49 ('89); 41 ('97) (this change may have taken place earlier; see Sch. II, 156); 77 ('06); and 85 ('15).

GOSSET *Paris*

Appears as a binder in 1809 at Galande 57, but by 1815–16 is listed as "gatherer only" and lived at No. 25.

GOTHSCHALK, *Maurice* *Paris*

Operated at Montmartre 84 from 1847–49.

GOUDOFFRE *Toulouse*

Worked in 1838 at Petite rue St. Rome and then at rue des Gestes 20 in 1847.

GOUFFE *Paris*

Noted at Petit-Bourbon 16 bis from 1847–49.

GOUIN *Nantes*

At rue des Carmes in 1828.

GOULBEAU

GOURDAINE *Nantes*

Rue du Moulin ('28); rue des Chapeliers ('29); Haute Grande rue ('30); No. 25 ('33).

GOUT, *Fils* *Montpellier*

Styles himself in 1839 as binder to the Musée Fabre. The only binding definitely connected with this "stationer and binder" is that cited and illustrated in Sch. II, 188. The binding, as a provincial one, seems contemporary with the date of the book, i.e. 1804. The address thereon is Barlerie 127, where he still worked when exhibiting at the Arts and Manufactures Exhibition at Montpellier in 1839. Subsequent addresses are: rue Aiguillerie and Place Notre Dame.

GOUX   *Chartres*

Noted in 1841.

GOUY, *Eugène*   *Paris*

Though apparently only active for twelve years, occupied various addresses as follows: Hotel Colbert 9 ('35); No. 7 ('42); St. Jacques 67 ('43); Parcheminerie 2 ('47).

GRABIE   *Toulouse*

At Place du Peyron in 1848.

GRAEL   *Paris*

This name in the 1832 Almanach is evidently, from the address, a mistake for Gruel.

GRARE   *Abbeville*

At rue de la Hucherie in 1826.

GRELAUD   *Nantes*

At rue des Etats, près du Château, 1841–48.

GRENET, J.   *Paris*

Sch. II, 108, illustrates a binding by him on a 1780 book of about contemporary style and the 1826 Almanach lists a binder of the same name (but without initials) at Godot 19. They may or may not be the same individual.

GRENIER, L.   *Paris*

The 1840 Almanach gives his address as Passage du Caire 78. When he moved to Passage St. Roch 15 in 1847, he added the initial "L".

GRESS

No details available.

GRETTEAU   *Bordeaux*

    Addresses: rue des Ayres ('36); rue du Hâ 12 ('48).

GRIESHABER, L.   *Strassburg*

    At rue-Neuve-quai des Bâteliers 9 in 1846.

GRISET, Fils Aîné   *Boulogne*

    His label, with address at Grand-Rue 682, figured on a *Language des Fleurs, c.* 1825–30, formerly in my own collection.

GRIZY   *Brionne*

    Only his place of work is known.

GROSCLAUDE, François (and bookseller)   *Metz*

    Born at Metz February 2, 1768 and set himself up in 1782 when his address was "au bas de la rue des Jardins". Later in 1818 he moved to Place St. Jacques. He died on February 25, 1835. Three of his works are described in Sch. III, Nos. 218–20, the first of which, illustrated therein, is now in my own collection. Each volume carries the interesting label.

GROSCLAUDE, Pierre-Napoleon   *Metz*

    Born at Metz May 7, 1808. Son of the above and also a binder.

GROSEAU   *Paris*

    Noted by the 1803 Almanach as at Noyers 42.

GRUEL (Gruel-Deforge), Pierre-Paul   *Paris*

    Béraldi states that he succeeded his father-in-law Deforge in 1825, but the first appearance of Gruel (misspelt Grael) which I have traced is in the 1832 Almanach at the Deforge address of Duphot 24. In 1835 he moved to Rue Royale 8, where he worked till at least 1847 as Gruel or Gruel-Deforge. The old firm of Deforge (*q.v.*) also continued to work at various addresses till 1849, and possibly Gruel was in some way still associated with it. The first Gruel died about 1848, and his widow (his second wife, formerly a Mlle. Mercier), who figures in the 1849 Almanach, married the printer J. Engelmann, in 1851. The present (1949) Gruel (Leon), now aged 86 is the grandson of the original Gruel. A portrait of Pierre-Paul Gruel drawn by himself in 1825 is in existence, and I am pleased to be able to reproduce it with his grandson's kind permission.

GUEDON   *Paris*

Appears in the 1797–98 Almanachs at Foin-St. Hilaire 2. A specimen of his work is illustrated in Rahir III, 831.

GUEFFIER   *Paris*

Resided at Galande 61 in 1815.

GUEFFIER, *Fils (and gilder)*   *Paris*

First in 1821 was at Hautefeuilles 14, and in 1826 at Guillemites 21. In 1832 he was gilder to the Mont-de-Piété, and to the Dépôts de la Marine et de la Ville. He is last mentioned in 1835.

GUEFFIER, *Veuve*   *Paris*

Noted at Galande 61 between 1797 and 1809.

GUEIGNEAU   *Paris*

Appears in the 1840–49 Almanachs at Grenelle 94.

GUERRINOT, *Jean-Etienne*   *Dijon*

He appears to have lived at Dijon between 1836 and 1840, at rue Portelle 50, rue de l'Ecole de Droit, and then at rue des Carmélites. He left Dijon about 1840, and may be the same as the Parisian binder noted below. He is reported to have specialised in half-bindings of great variety and good workmanship, while his full-bindings are said to be varied and original in style. I am glad to be able to reproduce a specimen through the courtesy of the Dijon librarian.

GUERRINOT   *Paris*

At Cambrai 9 from 1842–47.

GUETAN

Just a name noted.

GUICHERAT *Paris*

His address in 1843 was Vieille du Temple 92.

GUIDE-DOUTART *Amiens*

Worked at rue des Trois-Cailloux in 1826.

GUIGNARD

Romb. 42/43/A.695 reports a contemporary calf binding by the above on the Paulin *Molière*, 1835–36.

GUILLEMIN *Paris*

Appears in 1847–49 at St. Jacques 243 and Ursulines 10.

GUILLIEZ, E. *Paris*

The 1842–49 Almanachs give his address as Jacob 41.

GUITEL *Paris*

At St. Jean-de-Beauvais 24 in 1826.

GUTTERMANN, *Jacques* *Strassburg*

Noted in 1824 as at l'Hôpital 3.

GUYOT

He bound a copy of the 1834 Perrotin *Béranger* at about its date of issue (D. d'E.).

HAARHAUS *Paris*

His name appears on plates used for decorating the sides and spines of a number of books published about 1845, and issued in elaborately decorated cloth (and sometimes morocco) publisher's bindings. He sometimes signed these "plaques" in his own name and sometimes with that of Lenègre (*q.v.*) added. For specimens, see Maggs 661/252, 283, and 215. There seems no reason to think that he practised as a binder.

HALMBURGER *Lyons*

A specimen of his work is illustrated in Sch. III, 328. It is typically heavy work of about 1840–45. The label gives his address as Hôpital 54.

HALMBURGER, Antoine   *Lyons*

The Lyons Indicateurs of 1821–32 give his address as Place Confort 16.

HALMBURGER, George-Antoine   *Lyons*

The 1810 Indicateur gives his address as Place Confort 37, and he appears to have moved to No. 16 in 1816.

HALMBUGERE, François-Antoine   *Lyons*

Gruel I, p. 148, states that he resided at rue de l'Hôpital and was executed in 1793.

HAMELIN

See Rombaldi Guide du Bibliophile ('47) C.516, where a contemporary half-calf binding on a Lamartine collection (about 1825) is mentioned.

HAMERVILLE   *Paris*

The 1797–1803 Almanachs refer to him as at Sept Voies 16. Thoinan, on p. 312, refers to a Jacques-Guillaume of the same name as being received in 1759, working at rue Charretière in 1779, and still alive in 1790.

HAMERVILLE   *Chartres*

Address: Trois Maillets. (See Gruel ('05), II, p. 91.)

HANCKE, Louis   *Strassburg*

At La Croix 10 in 1824.

HARING   *Bordeaux*

In 1848 appears at Cours de Tournon 5.

HARMOIS   *Paris*

First at Plâtre 24 in 1832 and then at Montagne-Ste. Geneviève 29 from 1838–42.

HARMOIS, Jeune   *Paris*

At Montagne-Ste. Geneviève 1842–43.

HARTMANN, A.   *Strassburg*

Mentioned at Frères 24 in 1846.

HATTU, A.

Mentioned in Catalogue Vente J.H., April 1935, Giraud-Badin, No. 13.

HAUTOY, F. T.   *St. Quentin*

See Gruel I ('87), p. 110. His address was "Sur la Place" and he worked at the end of the eighteenth century.

HAVARD (*and gilder*)   *Paris*

At St. Jacques 134 in 1824.

HAVARD-ENGUERRAND   *Paris*

Almanachs 1843–47 give them as working at Charretière 7.

HEINGLE   *Lille*

The 1789 Lille Almanach mentions him at rue St. Maurice.

HELD, *Philippe-Jacques*   *Strassburg*

At Demi-Lune 3 in 1824.

HENNE

I noticed this signature in Paris, May 1949, on a book dated 1827. The binding appeared to be contemporary. He was still binding in 1838 (see Lardanchet's Cat. No. 44, Item 336).

HENRY   *Paris*

Mentioned in 1842 as at St. Séverin 16.

HERARD

No details beyond his name are available.

HERBEMONT

A fine calf binding (about 1821) by this binder is illustrated in Sch. III, No. 290. The ornamentation is mostly in effective blind-stamping.

HERBERT *Bordeaux*

At rue du Loup between 1789–92.

HERING *Paris*

The French binders of this name (they sometimes insert an acute accent on the first vowel of their name) present a number of problems, only less difficult of solution than those presented by their English contemporaries, though the name is prominent in England considerably earlier than in France.

Before attempting to deal in any detail with the "French" Herings individually, I can say that there was definitely a "J" and probably an "R". There was also a Hering "tout court", but who there is no reason to suppose was not, as the case might be, "J" or "R".

HERING, J. *Paris*

He appears in the 1826 Almanach with his initial, and I possess a binding signed J. Hering on the spine, covering the 1827 edition of Lesné's *La Reliure*. I have not been able to trace him or any other Hering working alone in the Almanachs of the epoch, except the ('26) Almanach, where his address is given as Buffault 22, and his work as "French and English", which would tend to indicate his close relationship (possibly family) with the London Herings, and to suggest that each branch on occasion supplied the other with bindings.

His other appearance in the Almanachs is in 1832, when the firm of J. Hering and F. Müller appears at Coquenard 24. I have not seen a specimen of the work of this combination with the relevant initials.

HERING, R.

The initial "R", though not recorded in the Almanachs, is said to occur on individual bindings, or on bindings signed R. Hering and Müller. The fact that he never appears to figure in the Almanachs, and the improbability that "J" can be responsible for all the Purgold-Hering, Hering and Müller combinations, and the assumption by Müller of the title of "Successor of Thouvenin", makes me wonder if the second Hering, be he "R" or not, was not an employee of Thouvenin. It would greatly help if one could trace an undoubted signature of "R" Hering. "R" may always be only short for "Relié par" (bound by).

HERING, G. *Strassburg*

He styled himself "Successor to Zabern", and was working at Fribourgeois 1 in 1846.

HERISSANT *Paris*

This binder figures in the Almanachs for nearly thirty years as follows: Charretière 4 ('97); Carmes 19 ('03); 24 ('15); St. Jacques 77 ('26).

HERISSANT, *Veuve* *Paris*

At Carmes 24 in 1821.

HERITIER *Paris*

Started about 1832 at St. Jacques 107; subsequently at 103 ('35); 29 ('40); 117 ('42–'49).

HERITIER, *Jeune* *Paris*

At St. Jacques 29 in ('43) and then at Noyers 25 in ('47). I have a nice rocaille binding by him about ('46).

HERLUISON *Orleans*

Worked at rue Faverie between 1832–46.

HEROS *Paris*

At St. Jean-de-Beauvais 13 in 1832.

HEROU *Paris*

Lesné ('27), p. 241, gives much praise to this producer of tools, especially for his excellent quality, large output, and quick delivery.

HERRMANN

Romb. 42// A.831 refers to a contemporary binding on a **Lafontaine** dated 1802.

HERSENT

A fine rocaille binding by him (about 1838) is described and illustrated in Jean Coulet's Cat. Spring 1949, No. 292.

HERVE   *Paris*

Worked at Vaugirard 6 from 1838–49.

HERVE   *Paris*

His address was Bièvre 33 from 1842–49.

HERVE   *Paris*

Is described as a stretcher and satiner, residing at Noyers 52 from 1842–49.

HERVOTTE

R.L.B. gives him as signing "binder-gilder" and working from 1825–35.

HERY   *Paris*

The 1832–42 Almanachs give his address as Zacharie 9.

HEUDE   *Paris*

Worked at Buffault 1 in 1847–49.

HEUDIER   *Paris*

Mentioned in Lesné ('27), p. 155, as an excellent washer and restorer of books. He appears in the 1803 Almanach at rue de la Harpe.

HIROU   *Paris*

According to the Almanachs he worked from 1826 at St. Jacques 150, and later 1840–43 at No. 142. Examples of his work are mentioned in the Rombaldi Guide of 1947, C. 511 and 674.

HITT

I also need information about him.

HODOST   *Paris*

Appears first in the 1797 Almanach at St. Jean-de-Beauvais 3 and lastly in 1815 at Plâtre-St. Jacques 12.

HOEFFEL, Chrétien-Charles   *Strassburg*

Worked in 1824 at Sanglier 6 and is mentioned in 1846 at No. 9, but apparently with the order of the Christian names reversed.

HORSCH, G.   *Strassburg*

At Arc-en-Ciel 11 in 1846.

HOUMANN   *Paris*

At Passage St. Roch 15 in 1842.

HUBERT   *Paris*

Shown at Suger 18 in 1847.

HUET, Edmond   *Le Mans*

Stated by M. Paul Cordonnier, Cons. de la Bibliothèque de la Ville du Mans, to have worked in 1846.

HUET-DESGRANGES   *Le Mans*

Stated by M. Paul Cordonnier to have been the brother of Edmond Huet (see above), and to have worked as stationer and binder from 1846–54.

HULIN   *Paris*

The Almanachs quote him at St. Jacques 55 in 1797–1803.

HULIN   *Paris*

First noted by me in the 1832 Almanach as at Montagne-Ste. Geneviève 52. He is probably the same as Hulin, Aîné, who worked at Carmes 5 from 1840–47.

HUNAULT   *Paris*

The 1842–49 Almanachs give him as at Harpe 13.

HUNDER(T)   *Bordeaux*

His first recorded address in 1807 is chez J. Foulquier et Cie. Pl. Royale 10. Sch. III, 236, describes and illustrates a contemporary binding by Hundert on an 1812 Bordeaux Calendar. His address is given as Trois-Conils 25 on his ticket; he appears to have worked here between 1811–16.

HUREZ, *Charles* *Cambra*

It is doubtful if this interesting binder falls within our period. Gruel ('05), II, p. 94, dates him as late as 1787. His address was rue de l'Arbre d'Or. In 1949 a Bournemouth bookseller had a curious specimen of his binding on Caraccioli's *Livre des Quatre Couleurs*, small 8-v.o full calf; the sides covered with four triangular inlays of red, green, yellow, and purple calf. In the centre of each cover, at the apex of the triangles, a gilt bee. Inside the front cover was a heart-shaped binder's ticket filled in in ink, similar to that illustrated by Gruel.

HURST, *Ch.* *Strassburg*

At Frères 15 in 1846.

IHRIG, *H.* *Paris*

Quoted in the 1840–49 Almanachs at Dauphine 26. Lardanchet's Paris shop had a fine specimen of his work in November 1949.

IPECH *Paris*

At Faubourg-St. Martin 185 between 1842–47.

ISECQ *Limoges*

Was at rue Manigne in 1836.

ISORE, *Etienne* *Paris*

Received in 1761, and lived at rue des Carmes in 1790.

ISSLER, *Jean* *Strassburg*

His address in 1824 was "derrière Temple-Neuf 11".

JACOB, *Charles-Nicolas* (*and bookseller*) *Metz*

Born at Metz in 1798. Established at rue de la Tête d'Or until 1857.

JACOTIER, *Louis-François* *Dijon*

Lived at St. Martin 20 between 1822–32. He may have started work somewhat earlier, as Sch. 281 describes and illustrates a binding on a biography of Bossuet, dated 1819, which appears slightly earlier in style. The Dijon Library reports three bindings by him in their possession, which show tools similar to those used by Mairet, whose pupil Jacotier may have been.

JACOTIER   *Paris*

This binder of St. Antoine 178 received a bronze medal for his invention for copying prints and lithographs on bindings, etc., in 1834. He may be the same as L.-F. J. above, as a Jacotier of Paris showed at the Dijon Arts Exhibition in 1837.

JACQUELIN, Fils   *Paris*

At Marais du Temple 12 in 1847.

JACQUELIN   *Limoges*

At rue du Verdurier in 1836.

JACQUET   *Paris*

Thoinan, p. 316 (see *Jaquez*), states that a Jacquet was working in 1810 at rue Guisarde 15, where the 1815 Almanach locates him. Thoinan hints that he may be the same as Jean-Julian Jaquez, received in 1767, and living at rue des Amandiers.

JACQUINOT   *Paris*

At Lavoisier 3 in 1847.

JAGER   *Lyons*

The Lyons Indicateur of 1813 gives him at Place du Port du Temple 43.

JAGER, Charles-Marie-Gabriel   *Lyons*

Noted at Thomassin 62 in 1810.

JAGER   *Paris*

First at Noyers 4 in 1838 and then at Galande 45 in 1840.

JAMET   *Paris*

Worked at St. Honoré 73 in 1836–38.

JANDEL   *Paris*

Appears in the 1803 Almanach at Sept-Voies 13 and finally at Rheims 4 in 1815.

JANDELLE   *Paris*

   1826–49 at various addresses: St. Jacques 134 ('26); Charretière 9 ('42);
   St. Jean-de-Beauvais 11 ('42); 16 ('49).

JANET, Pierre-Etienne   *Paris*

   Received in 1776 when he lived at rue St. Jean-de-Beauvais; in 1785
   he moved, according to Thoinan, p. 316, to rue Charretière. About
   1792 he went to rue St. Jacques, where he may have lived till 1818.
   He was brother-in-law to J. P. Jubert, whom he succeeded in 1792.
   He continued the ephemeral bindings, and possibly developed the
   equally ephemeral publication side of the business, later so prominent
   a feature of the production of Louis Janet. The binding described
   and illustrated in Sch. II, 208, is probably a sound example of this
   side of his work.

JANET, Fils   *Paris*

   An olive green morocco binding, so signed, belonging to Pauline
   Borghese, seen at Maggs in December 1947, may be the work of
   Louis Janet while still working with his father.

JANET, Louis (sometimes styled "Jeune")   *Paris*

   Appears in the Almanachs at St. Jacques 57 in 1815; 61 in ('16);
   and 59 in ('26–'42). Thoinan, p. 316, claims that he succeeded his
   father and moved to St. Jacques 59 in ('19). His long career as a
   publisher of ephemera is well known, but can be studied further in
   Grand-Carteret's *Almanachs Français* 1896.

JANET, Veuve L.   *Paris*

   Apparently continued her late husband's business at St. Jacques 59
   from 1843–49.

JANET   *Paris*

   Makes an appearance at Mail 33 in 1847.

JAPIN, F. A. L.   *Amsterdam*

   Mr. Percy Muir reports a binding (about 1844) with a label "Relié
   par/ F.A.L. Japin/ à Amsterdam". He was probably French by
   origin.

JAROT   *Paris*

Appears at Carmes 23 in 1821, and finally at Amandiers 5 in 1842.

JAROT, Fils   *Paris*

Also at Amandiers 5 in 1843.

JARREAU   *Paris*

In 1815 he was domiciled at Carmes 23.

JAUJON   *Montpellier*

Exhibited in the Montpellier Exhibition in November 1839. His
address was Maison René.

JEAN (gilder)   *Paris*

Cited in Lesné ('20) (the earlier edition).

JEANNEAU   *Nantes*

Addresses: Quai St. Jean Barth 3 ('41); rue Rameau 3 ('44); rue de la
Perouse ('45).

JEASSEM   *Bordeaux*

At rue Voltaire 7 in 1836.

JENIVEAU   *Bordeaux*

Worked between 1807–19 at rue St. James 17.

JENOTTE   *Paris*

At Madeleine 23/25 from 1840–43.

JOIREZ   *Boulogne*

The 1846–48 *Boulogne Annual* gives him as at Siblequin 18.

JOLIVET   *Paris*

Prêtres-St. Germain 3 in 1840–43.

JOLLY   *Paris*

Appears in the 1840 Almanach at Voltaire 12, and finally at Sept
Voies 13 in 1847.

JOLY   *Lille*

Rue du Pont-Neuf 5 ('35); 20 ('37); 18 ('38–'48).

JOUBLIN   *Paris*

Practised between 1826 and 1849, first at Grands Augustins 24, then
at Eperons 3 in 1832, and from 1842 onwards at Mathurins 15.

JOUILLARD   *Péronne*

His address in 1826 was: Sur la Place.

JOURNEAUX   *Paris*

First worked at St. Jean-de-Beauvais 29 in 1842, from whence he
moved in 1849 to Bernardins 34.

JOUVENEZ   *Lille*

The Lille Almanach 1788–89 gives his address as rue des Vieux-Murs.

JOUY

J. Rousseau-Girard's Cat. 10, No. 3847, mentions a blind-stamped
rocaille calf binding by him dating about 1838.

JOYAL   *Clermont*

Signed a work dated 1826, see Cat. Lascoutx, I.462.

JOZON *and* CHAUVET   *Paris*

The 1832 Almanach gives their address as Neuve des Petits-Champs
29. Sch. III, 297, describes and illustrates what appears to be a rather
sophisticated type of Gothic or "cathedral" mosaic binding on an
1824 Paroissien.

JUBEAU (*Jubeau-Royné* after 1848)   *Angers*

At rue Baudrière between 1840–48.

JUBERT   *Paris*

His career, which hardly falls within the period of this study, is dealt with at considerable length by Thoinan, p. 318. He was received in 1777, and was very well known as a binder and seller of all sorts of ephemera of the period. He lived at rue St. Jacques (? No. 37), and passed his business over in 1792 to his brother-in-law, P.-E. Janet (*q.v.*).

JUGUET (or JUGUET-BUSSEUIL)   *Nantes*

Addresses: Place Bourbon ('25); Place du Pilori ('31–'37).

JUNDT, Jean-Jacques   *Strassburg*

At Hallebardes 8 in 1824.

JUSTE   *Paris*

Started at Montagne-Ste. Geneviève 52 in 1826, and moved in 1832 to Fossés-St. Victor 2, where he worked till 1836.

KALENBACK   *Paris*

According to Bér. Rel. I, p. 34, was at 4 rue Chabanais in 1814.

KALENKI (see KERN).

KAMM, Daniel   *Strassburg*

At Vieux-marché-aux-poissons 17 in 1824.

KAUFMANN   *Paris*

At Seine 9 according to the 1847–49 Almanachs.

KERN and KALENKI

Late binders of the period.

KETTNER, F.   *Strassburg*

At Juifs 9 in 1846.

KILCHER   *Paris*

Lesné ('27), p. 241, refers to his special facility for preparing tools for lettering.

KISIEL   *? Paris*

My collection contains a half-morocco binding signed at base of spine by Kisiel on *La Pologne Illustrée*, Paris 1839–41. It is a typical binding of the period, and carries the Polish and Lithuanian emblems. I feel confident that it was bound in Paris by a Polish refugee of the period.

KLEBERT   *Nantes*

At rue Beau-Soleil in 1847–48.

KLEINHANS   *Paris*

Appears regularly in the 1815–49 Almanachs, first at Guénégaud 15, and then from 1826 at Mazarine 56. Béraldi Rel. I, p. 34, gives his address in 1814 at Guénégaud 33. Was Trautz's first employer in Paris. My own collection has an excellent binding executed about 1840 for Louis Philippe in full morocco with the latter's monogram on the sides.

KNECHT, Ch.   *Strassburg*

At Epine 7 in 1846.

KNECHT, Jean-Nepomucène   *Strassburg*

Appears at Fossé des Tailleurs 9 in 1824.

KOCK, Th.   *Paris*

At Montorgueil 15 from 1847–49.

KOEHLER, F.   *Paris*

A first-class binder, of whom one would like to know more. What we roughly do know is that he started on his own at Ancienne Comédie 12 by 1834; moved to Bac 75 in ('40), and two years later to Grenelle 59, where he remained at least till 1849. While he sometimes produced hack-work, most of his production was on restrained lines. He was a pupil of Thoivenin, and succeeded to much of his work. He was awarded an "A" Medal in 1834 and 1839, and still one does not quite know where to place him, or where to point to his best work. Desc. Nos. 200 and 424 are his work, but one feels that he must somewhere have achieved a masterpiece that we have not yet seen.

KOENIG, *Charles-Louis*   *Strassburg*

Worked at Ste. Barbe 4 from 1824–46.

KOENIGS, *Edouard*   *Paris*

Worked at Quai St. Michel 11 from 1847–49.

KORN, *Th.*   *Strassburg*

At same address, and probably the same as T. Corn (*q.v.*).

KOSTELEVZKI

My own collection has a binding by him on a 3-volume work dated
1823, with which it is roughly contemporary.

KRAUSS, *D.*   *Strassburg*

At rue de l'Hôpital in 1846.

KRONHEIM

A designer of tools, whose work is illustrated in Maggs 661/247,
263. Working about 1845.

KUMMERLEN, *Théophile*   *Strassburg*

Worked at La Lie 9 in 1824, and later in 1846 was at No. 5.

LABOURE, *Etienne*   *Paris*

At St. Lazare 16 in 1835, and at St. Jean-de-Beauvais 20 in the
following year.

LABREVEUX   *Paris*

The Almanachs show him at St. Jean-de-Beauvais 30 in 1832; at
No. 24 in ('35); at 40 in ('47); and at Anglais 8 in 1849. Maggs in
September 1948 reported a ticket by him on Florian's Works,
published 1829.

LACAUVE, *Jacques-François*   *Paris*

According to Thoinan, p. 320, he was received in 1775. He appears
in the 1797–1803 Almanachs, and resided at Mont-St. Hilaire 9.

LACAUVE, Jeune   *Paris*

According to Thoinan, p.320, he was the son of Jacques-François. He appears in the 1809–26 Almanachs, at Mont-St. Hilaire 4.

LACHAPELLE   *Strassburg*

At Juifs 45 in 1846.

LACORNEE, Joseph   *Paris*

Born 1815, died 1880. Address: Savoie 11. (Gruel 18/7/49.)

LACOSTE, de   *Nantes*

Addresses: Quai Cossard ('28); aux Petits Murs ('29); Place St. Vincent ('33–'37).

LACOSTE

He is mentioned as a contemporary binder of Dupont: *Œuvres Pastorales* 1837 in Rombaldi: Guide 44.G.171.

LACOUR   *Paris*

The Almanach Typographique 1799 mentions him at |St. Jean-de-Beauvais.

LACOUTURE   *? Paris*

My own collection contains a contemporary "mourning" binding by him on *Passion de Jésus-Christ* 1843. Maggs 661/223 is also by him, and the initials "L.C." are probably his and not those of L. Curmer.

LACROIX   *Paris*

Working at St. Jean-de-Beauvais in 1799 according to the Almanach Typographique.

LACY   *Paris*

First at Place de l'Etoile 6 in 1840, and then at Chevalier du Guet 3 from 1847–49.

LAFERTE, Pierre-Louis II   *Paris*

Thoinan, p. 321, states that he was received in 1761, and then lived at rue des Carmes. He moved to rue d'Ecosse in 1779, and was still working in 1790.

LAFERTE, François   *Paris*

Also worked at rue des Carmes, 1761–90.

LAFERTE, Joseph-Louis-Antoine   *Paris*

Thoinan, p. 322, says that he was received in 1773, and lived at rue des Amandiers, and later in 1779 at rue Galande. He is probably the same as the one working 1800–04 at St. Jean-de-Beauvais 32.

LAFERTE (gilder)   *Paris*

Lesné ('27), p. 90, refers to him, as also to Noël and Leprince, as using their gold much too thinly.

LAFOND   *Paris*

Quoted in the 1797–98 Almanach as at St. Jean-de-Beauvais 7.

LAGARDE (and stationer)   *Marseilles*

Was at rue Vacon 18 from 1827 and then between 1844–48 at No. 28.

LAGIER

Mentioned in Cat. 11, Item 4641, of J. Rousseau-Girard (about 1948).

LAGNY   *Paris*

See Thoinan, p. 322. He was first at rue d'Ecosse 4 in 1803, and six years later at No. 8.

LAGNY   *Paris*

See Thoinan, p. 322. First noted at Mignon 1 in 1803, then at Deux-Portes St. André 7 in 1809, and finally between 1816–21 at Cloître St. Benoit 8.

LAGNY, Jeune   *Paris*

Worked at Mathurins in 1799 and at Sept-Voies 3 in 1815.

LAGORCE   *Limoges*

Master-binder between 1720(?)–89.

LAINE, Marc-Antoine-Charles-Guillaume   *Paris*

He was received in 1767 and lived at rue des Amandiers. According to Thoinan, he was still active up to 1810. In that case he may be the Lainé who figures in the Almanachs as follows: Amandiers 7 ('03); 10 ('09); St. Jean-de-Beauvais 30 ('21); Clovis 10 ('26).

LAINE   *Paris*

At St. Martin 101 in 1842.

LAISNEY   *Peronne*

Between 1826–27 his address was: Sur la Place.

LAJANNIERE   *Paris*

The 1821 Almanach mentions him at Grès 2.

LALANDE   *Paris*

Worked at Beauvais 14 in 1798, and may have been still active up to 1811, as the Brouwet Cat. May '35, No. 43, gives his signature on a book of that date. The Almanach Typographique 1799 mentions a Lalande at St. Jean-de-Beauvais.

LALANDE, Mme.   *Paris*

At Noyers 37 in 1803.

LALANDE (later *DESPIERRES*)   *Paris*

First appears in 1815 at Rats 14 and then 1832–38 at Grands Augustins 10. Sch. III, 293, describes and illustrates a typical calf binding of the date (about 1822) mostly in blind-stamp.

LALLEMAND   *Paris*

Working at St. Jean-de-Beauvais 20 in 1815–16.

LALLEMAND, Pierre-Jacques   *Paris*

According to Thoinan, p. 322, was received in 1768, and resided at rue St. Jacques. The 1803 Almanach mentions a binder of this name at No. 644. The 1799 Almanach Typographique mentions this binder and another of the same name at Cloître Benoit.

117

LAMBERT *Paris*

A binder of this name appears at Harpe 66 in 1835; another or the same at Plâtre St. Jacques 22 in 1838–40. In 1842 there seem to have been two Lamberts at No. 11 and No. 20 St. Jean-de-Beauvais respectively.

LAMBERT, A. *? Nancy*

This binder's name appears on an 1821 Nancy breviary in my own collection. D. d'E. reports bindings at least as late as 1842.

LAMPES, F. *Strassburg*

At Charpentiers 24 in 1846.

LANGLES

Mentioned in the Duchesse de Berry Cat. as the binder of Item 1277.

LANGLOIS *Paris*

Mentioned by Thoinan, p. 324, and figures in the 1797–1826 Almanachs as follows: Charretière 6, 1797; Amandiers 7, 1800; St. André-des-Arts 26 ('15); Macon 8 ('26).

LANGLOIS *Nantes*

Started at Racine 2 ('04); then rue Voltaire ('17); Haut de la rue Racine ('25); rue Contrescarpe ('28–'37). There was an earlier binder of the same name at Lyons (see Sch. II, 110/1).

L'ANGLOIS, Adrien *Chartres*

He signs at foot of spine a delightfully plain binding in my possession on Paris-Londres ('37). The end-papers show his name and Chartres on the watermark.

LANGLOIS, François

R.L.B. reports a binder of this name as working between 1815 and 1826.

LANNE

See Rombaldi 42/43/A.724. He may have worked about 1819, but signatures are reported as late as 1838.

LANNES   *Paris*

Appears in the 1847-9 Almanachs at Dauphine 48.

LANTERNIER, Jean-Claude (and bookseller)   *Metz*

Born at Gorze (Moselle) in 1792. Worked from 1831 at rue du Porte-Enseigne (rue Serpenoise) and after 1844 at Place Napoléon (place d'Armes).

LAPEYRIERE   *Paris*

Worked at Seine 9 in 1847–49.

LARCHIER   *Lyons*

The Lyons Indicateur gives him at Grande rue Mercière 51 in 1842.

LARCHIER, Jean   *Lyons*

Appears at Grande rue Mercière 59 in 1810, and at No. 51 from 1813–16.

LARCHIER, Pierre   *Lyons*

Worked at Grande rue Mercière 54 in 1821.

LARD-ESNAULT   *Paris*

The 1843–49 Almanachs give his address as Feydeau 23.

LARDIERE (see Thompson)   *Paris*

The 1840 Almanach gives his address as Louis-le-Grand 35; from 1842–49 he appears to have been at No. 30. He received a bronze medal in 1839.

LARDIN   *Paris*

First at St. Jean-de-Beauvais 13 in 1840, and then at No. 11 from 1842-43.

LAROCHE, Medard   *Dijon*

At 2 rue St. Pierre in 1836.

LARRIVIERE, J. N. *Lille and Paris*

He probably started about 1820, and is noted at rue de la Clef, Lille, in 1829. He first appears in the Paris Almanachs about 1842, which may mean that he was primarily a Lille binder, his Paris address from 1842–49 being 3 and 15 rue Aumâle and Gravilliers 38. He achieved on occasion really outstanding work by means chiefly of deep blind-stamping executed mostly with individual hand tools. A binding on Buscone's Architecture 1590 in my own collection is a good example of this kind of work. Another excellent example of his work is illustrated in Desc. II, 206, and shows that he was operating from Lille as King's binder in 1828. The binding illustrated in Maggs 661/72 is less striking.

LARRIVIERE *Bordeaux*

At rue des Gourgues 2 ('07–'11) and rue St. James 27 ('19).

LARROUX *Bordeaux*

At Cours de Tourny between 1836–39.

LARTET *Toulouse*

At rue du Peyron 1837–47.

LARTIGUE *Toulouse*

From 1807–38 at rue Fourbastard.

LASSALLE *Paris*

Worked at Mont-St. Hilaire 6 from 1832–39.

LASSALLE *Agen*

He appears to have worked about 1840, judging from the rocaille style of the half-morocco binding illustrated in Sch. III, 309.

LATOUCHE *Bordeaux*

Worked at rue Neuve 17, 1791–92; rue du Parlement 30, 1807–11.

LATOUR *Toulouse*

At rue Fourbastard 16, 1833–48.

LATOUR-FOUQUET   *Nantes*

Worked at Contrescarpe 54 ('43–'48).

LAURENCY   *Paris*

Appears in the 1838–42 Almanachs at Neuve St. Martin 30.

LAURENT   *Paris*

Noted at Coquillière 29 in 1842–43, though he may have worked earlier. Specimens of his work appear in Bér. Cat. III, 181 and 232, and in Romb. 42/43.A.695.

LAURIN, Jean-François-Claude   *Lyons*

The Lyons Indicateur 1821 gives him as at l'Hôpital 14.

LAVERONIERE   *? Paris*

All that is known of him is that Lesné ('27), p. 35, mentions him as a doughty champion ("preux") of solidity in binding.

LAVIGNAC   *Bordeaux*

At rue Porte-Basse 6 ('07–'16).

LE BASTARD   *Nantes*

At rue de la Commune between 1828–31.

LE BATTEUX   *Le Mans*

Probably worked between 1830–40. He received a Bronze Medal at the 1836 (? Paris) Exhibition, which is quoted on his ticket on a binding in my collection on a Le Mans publication dated 1838.

LEBIGRE

LEBLANC   *Limoges*

At rue du Verdurier in 1836 and rue Puy-Vieille-Monnaie in 1846.

LEBLOIS   *Limoges*

Master-binder 1766–89.

LEBRETON *Paris*

Appears in 1826 at Foin-St. Germain 28.

LEBRUN *Paris*

A very competent, but rather dull, binder. He probably started about 1830, was favourably quoted in the 1839 Exhibition, received a Bronze Medal in 1844, and specialised in backs "à la grotesque" (see Sch. III, 326). He appears in the 1840–49 Almanachs at Grenelle 126, and was still working in 1851.

LECLER *Bayonne*

Worked between 1840–50 at Bourg Neuf 68.

LECLER, Prosper (and gilder) *Paris*

The 1826 Almanach quotes him as at Childebert 11. S. de Ricci believed that the binding illustrated in Sch. III, 314, dates about 1830.

LECLERC *Paris*

Worked from 1840–47 at Neuve-Ste. Geneviève 4.

LECLERC *Paris*

At Mouffletard 97 between 1840–49.

LECLERC *Paris*

Noted at Abbaye 1 in 1821.

LECLERC *Paris*

His addresses were as follows: St. Benoit 18 ('35); 10 ('42); 8 ('43); Sts. Pères 47 ('47).

LECLERCQ *Lille*

At rue Royale 54 in 1848.

LECRENE

The only binding by him known to me is in my own collection on *Les Pèlerins*, published anonymously at Falaise in 1807. It is in full morocco gilt, with green silk "tabis" and appears strictly contemporary.

LEDANOIS   *Paris*

Appears at Rempart 969 in 1797–98.

LEDANOIS (and gilder)   *Paris*

The 1821–26 Almanachs give his address as Parcheminerie 2, and
Lesné refers to him as one of the three best gilders of his time.

LEDOUX, F. R.   *Paris*

Quoted in the 1826–38 Almanachs, and may have worked earlier.
He was capable of excellent work. I have only a small half-calf
binding of his. The following were his addresses: Bertin Poirée 6
('26); Bac 134 ('32); Grenelle 126 ('35). One of his bindings is reproduced in Béraldi's *Estampes et Livres*.

LEFEBVRE   *Paris*

According to Thoinan, p. 327, he was nephew or son-in-law of one
or other of the Bozérians. He is noted in the 1809–26 Almanachs,
first at Quai des Augustins 27 and in 1826 at rue St. Christophe 10.
His best work was done in co-operation with Bozérian (see Bozérian
and Lefebvre). Much, though not all, of his own work was hack work
of the Bozérian type. Samples are fairly easy to come across, e.g.
Sch. II, 201/206; Gum. 348; Rahir III, 838.

LEFEVRE   *? Paris*

Lesné ('27), pp. 99, 241, and 375, refers to him as an excellent producer
of small binders' ornamental stamps and tools.

LEFEVRE   *Paris*

Listed at Passage de la Réunion 10 from 1843–49.

LEFORT   *Paris*

His address seems to have been rue Thiroux, section de la Place des
Piques, ci-devant Vendôme (? about 1793–98; see Gruel '05, II,
p. 105). Also spelt himself "Le For". A Lefort appears in the Almanach
Typographique 1799 at Place du Théâtre Italien.

LEFRERE   *Paris*

At Ecosse 4 in 1797.

LEFUEL *Paris*

Appears in the 1803–09 Almanachs at St. Jacques 27 and 54 respectively. I have seen a fine yellow morocco binding, with blue inlays in Bozérian's best style, and signed by Lefuel at the base of the spine, at Gaillandre's shop in Paris in 1949.

LEFUEL, *Fils* *Paris*

I have only noticed him recorded once in the Almanachs as a binder, i.e., in 1826, when he was at Seine 36.

LEGER *Paris*

Appears between 1815–26 as follows: Neuve-des-Bons-Enfants 33–35 ('15); Harpe 17 ('16); Petit-Pont 5 ('21); Bièvre 22 ('26).

LEGRAVERANT *Paris*

Worked at Faubourg St. Martin 22 from 1847–49.

LEGROS *Nantes*

Started at rue Nicolas in 1825; was at rue Royale in 1838, where he also dealt as a bookseller.

LEGROS *Orleans*

At Marché St. Etienne in 1846.

LEGROS *Paris*

Cited as working at Macon 10 from 1835–43.

LEHOUX *Nantes*

Addresses: rue Beau-Soleil ('28); Carmélites ('30–'32).

LEHRNER *? Vienne*

LEIDLER *Amiens*

Noted in 1826 at Cloître Notre Dame 4.

LEJARD *Paris*

At Porte St. Honoré 2 in 1832.

LEMAIRE, *Aîné* *Paris*

Recorded from 1832–49 at Passage du Commerce St. André 13.

LEMOINE, *Jean* *Le Mans*

According to a note received from M. Paul Cordonnier, Keeper of the Le Mans Library, he was working in 1830.

LEMOINE, *Jean-Jacques (and second-hand books)* *Metz*

Born at Dunkirk about 1750. Set up in 1785 at rue St. Clement, and then in 1815 at rue Ponteffroy.

LEMONNIER, *Antoine-Joseph* *Paris*

According to Thoinan, p. 333, he was received in 1763, and still working in 1790. His first address was rue St. Jean-de-Beauvais, and from 1779, St. Jacques 196.

LEMONNIER *Paris*

First noted in 1797 at Sept Voies 17, and then at No. 31 from 1809–21.

LEMONNIER *Paris*

Started in 1797 at Mont. Hilaire 3, then at Charretière 5 in 1803 and No. 9 in 1815–16.

LEMONNIER *Paris*

First noted in 1803 at St. Jean-de-Beauvais 3, and then in 1809 at St. Jacques 103.

LEMONNIER *? Paris*

Lesné mentions him as one of the best gilders of his day, and as having retired in 1820. The firm then seems to have become Lemonnier Chesle.

LEMONNIER, *Veuve* *Paris*

Occurs in the 1826 Almanach at Sept-Voies 31.

LEMPRUN, *Nicolas* *Paris*

The Almanachs give his addresses as: Carmes 19 ('97); 12 ('03); 23 ('15–21). See also Thoinan, p. 336.

LENEGRE   *Paris*

The business claimed in 1880 to have been founded in 1839, and it appears in the 1842–49 Almanachs at the following addresses: Furstemberg 11 ('42); Abbaye 4 ('43); St. Germain des Près 11 bis ('47). Examples of his work are common. (See for examples Maggs 661/194, 282.)

LENEGRE *et* HAARHAUS   *Paris*

In this combination, which worked about 1845–47, there seems no doubt that Lenègre was the binder and Haarhaus the designer of the engraved plates used on the sides and spine of the bindings. For a specimen see Maggs 661/215.

LENEGRE-SOUZA   *Paris*

? after period.

LENFANT, G.

A very competent calf binding, with small printed label, seen in Amsterdam (1949). Probable date about 1826.

LENFANT, *Veuve*   *Lille*

At rue Grande-Chaussée 52 in 1840–42.

LENOIR, *Léon*   *Lyons*

Mentioned in the Lyons Almanach for 1810 at Grande rue Mercière, maison Bégule 45 bis and in 1813 at No. 61. An example of his work, which may well be anterior to 1810, is illustrated in Sch. III, 235.

LENOIR, *Léonard*   *Lyons*

The Lyons Indicateur for 1821 gives his address as Passy 3.

LENOIR, *Louis*   *Lyons*

At Grande rue Mercière 16 from 1815–16.

LENOIR, *Veuve*   *Lyons*

Stated to have worked at Passy 3 in 1832. May have been the widow of *Léonard*.

LENOIR-MOREL   *Angers*

> At rue St. Michel from 1840–48.

LENORMAND, L-Sébastien   *Paris*

> Himself a binder, he published a *Manuel de Relieur* in 1827. (See *Berthe*.)

LEON-FIXON   *Paris*

> He is stated to have been a pupil of Thouvenin and worked at Montorgueil 33 from 1835–49.

LEOPOLD   *Paris*

> His address 1797–98 was Galande 61.

LEOPOLD-GRENIER   *Paris*

> Noted at Passage St. Roch 37 in 1842–47.

LEPAGE, Arthur   *Paris*

> From 1847–49 he worked at St. Honoré 385.

LEPRE (Pupil of Doll)   *Nantes*

> At Haute Grande-rue 19 ('29); rue du Briord ('48). A fine example of his work on a 4-volume Breviary, having belonged to a former archbishop of Nantes, was at E. Rossignol's in 1950.

LEPRINCE, P.   *Paris*

> Active from 1803–47, as follows: Charretière 17 ('03); 4 ('15); St. Hilaire 8 ('32); Amandiers 13 ('47). He is said to have bound chiefly in basil, and to have been stingy with his gold. (See Lesné ('27), pp. 90, 290, 335.)

LEPRINCE, Paul   *Amiens*

> This Amiens business man decided in the 1820s to undertake the binding of the 500 or so manuscripts round which the Amiens town library has been built. The MSS. came from the religious houses of the region, and had unfortunately been stripped of their bindings at the time of the revolution. Leprince went specially to Paris to learn the art of binding. On his return to Amiens about 1828 he set to work

to bind the 500 MSS. in question "with care and elegance" (to quote the words of the Keeper of the Amiens Library, to whose courtesy I owe this and much other valuable information).

LEROUX — *Paris*

Appears at Bourbon-Villeneuve 5 in 1835 and at Ponceau 1 the following year.

LEROUX-KLEBERT (*see KLEBERT*) — *Nantes*

Rue des Saintes-Claires ('25); Haute Grande-rue ('33–'37).

LEROUX, Ferd-X — *Strassburg*

At Sainte-Hélène 14 in 1846.

LEROUX, *Veuve* — *Montdidier*

Worked at Place de la Croix Bleue in 1826.

LEROY, Ch. — *Boulogne*

The Boulogne Annuals given him as working at Farinette 28 between 1843–48. A note from the Municipal Library indicates that from work C.6752 there he may have been active as early as 1821.

LEROYNY — *Paris*

Appears at Amandiers 7 in 1803.

LERVE — *Paris*

Worked successively at St. Jacques 22 ('36); Parcheminerie 2 ('38); Noyers 52 ('42).

LESAGE — *Paris*

Noted at Hotel-Colbert 16 in 1842.

LESCLAPART — *Paris*

Shown between 1797 and 1803 as at Ecosse 3.

LESNE, Mathurin-Marie   *Paris*

Thoinan, pp. 339–40, gives a succinct account of his career, and Béraldi's *Reliure au XIXᵉ Siècle* devotes much space to this very competent binder, but still more to his poem on Binding, which, whatever its value as poetry, is an invaluable guide to the French binders and the binding practice of the first quarter of the nineteenth century.

I have little to add to the above accounts, save a note on his very numerous addresses. According to Béraldi, he started to bind in 1804, but his first authenticated address seems to be at Grès 5 in 1819 and then at Harpe 78 in 1821. Some time before 1819 he may have worked at rue d'Enfer. Thereafter his addresses were as follows: Tournon 19 ('26); Ouest 95 ('32); St. Denis 258 and St. Jacques 256 ('35); Odéon 25 ('38); Petit Léon 17 ('40). The business was apparently carried on after his tragic death by drowning in 1841, first at Clichy 17 ('42), and then at Vivienne 12 ('43). He was the recipient of a "B" mention in 1834. Illustrations of his work can be found in Maggs 661/268, Bér. Rel. plate 25 (facing p. 70), and Bér. Cat. V, 178.

LESNE, Jeune   *Paris*

His only appearance in the Almanachs seems to be in 1836, when he was at Vaugirard 17. His father dedicated the first (1820) edition of *La Reliure* to him, and on p. 328 of the ('27) edition refers to his apprenticeship with Thouvenin who, Lesné infers, did not pay too much attention to his training, cp. Letter to Kleinhans in Bér. Rel. I, facing p. 82.

A binding by him is described and illustrated in Sch. III, 305. The volume in question is dated 1826, and the Lesné *F* in question may well have been binding on his own at that date.

LESORT

His signature figures on a work dated 1844 (see B. de F. 295).

LESPES   *Bayonne*

Noted as a stationer and binder at Port Mayon about 1840–50.

LESTRINGANT   *Paris*

Figures in the 1836–49 Almanachs at St. Jean-de-Latran 9.

LESUEUR   *Montdidier*

   Worked at rue Parmentier in 1826.

LETELLIER, *Louis-Nicolas*   *Paris*

   According to Thoinan, p. 341, he was received in 1766, when he
   lived at rue des Chiens. Subsequently in 1779 he was at rue des
   Amandiers, and is very possibly the same as the binder of the 98–99
   Almanach living at rue des Sept-Voies.

LETEURTRE   *Boulogne*

   His address was "sur la place, haute-ville". I have a nice morocco
   binding with his label on a book dated 1825, and from other bindings
   of his, which I have seen, I should place his activity at about 1820–30.

LEVACHER   *Orleans*

   At rue de la Crosse in 1832, and later in 1846 at rue de Mes Chevaux.

LEVASSEUR, *Adolphe*   *Marseilles*

   This binder worked first in 1841 as Levasseur et Cie., and then in
   1843 as Levasseur et Michel, in both cases at rue de la Palud 25.
   In 1844 he was working at Vacon 28 as Levasseur, and later at rue
   de Rome 46 ('46) and rue de la Darce 1 ('47).

LEVASSEUR, *Aîné*   *Marseilles*

   Worked at rue Mazade 1 in 1848. May have been the same as *Adolphe*
   (*q.v.*).

LEVASSEUR, *Jeune*   *Marseilles*

   Working at rue de la Palud in 1845. The Communal Archives of
   Marseilles contain a blue velvet binding, signed by him, on the
   1848 Constitution.

LEVRAT, *François*   *Lyons*

   The Lyons Indicateur for 1842 mentions him at Tupin 22.

LEZ   *Paris*

   At Université 42 in 1832, and at Lille 23 from 1838–47.

L'HOSTE-MARÇON   *Paris*

Worked at St. Denis 371 in 1826.

LHUER

Worked about 1842.

LIBERMANN   *Paris*

The Almanachs 1832–49 give his address as Mazarine 16. My own
collection has a calf binding on a '28 Psautier, with the same blind
stamping as a later Capé binding also in my collection. (See also
Maggs 661/173 and 213, both rocaille, and later in date than my
own specimen.)

LIBERT-PETITOT   *Lille*

At Place du Théâtre 47 between 1838–41. His widow seems to have
had charge from 1840.

LICHAGUE   *Toulouse*

Addresses: Rue des Gestes ('33); rue du Taur ('47–'48).

LIEVRAIN   *Amiens*

Working in 1826 at Basse-rue Notre Dame.

LIGOT   *Orleans*

At rue de l'Aiguillerie in 1846.

LINIUS, *Père*   *? Paris*

E. Fournier, *Art de la Reliure* ('88), described him as the teacher of
Thouvenin, in which case he may have been employed at the atelier
of Bozérian Jeune.

LODIGIANI   *Milan*

Though not a French binder, I have included Lodigiani on account
of his work for Napoleon I, and the close connection of his style
with that of French binders of the same date. The tickets I have seen
call him "Relieur de S.A.I.", i.e. His Imperial Highness. For illustrations of his work see Sch. IV, 75, and Gum. 326 and 327.

LONGRE, Pierre *Paris*

According to Thoinan, p. 343, he was received in 1765 and lived at rue d'Ecosse. He was still working in 1803 at Charretière 6.

LONGRE (edge-gilder) *Paris*

See PIERRY, Mme.

LOR(R)ILL(I)ARD, Pierre *Dijon*

Son of Jean Lorilliard (baker) and Cathérine Perrie. Born July 27, 1800 at Dijon, and died, unmarried, September 17, 1836 at petite rue du Morimont. He was the favourite pupil and successor of Mairet, who strongly recommended him before his (Mairet's) retirement in 1821. He first lived with Mairet, and then in 1824 at Place St. Georges. The Dijon Library possesses several specimens of his work. Lorilliard appears to have helped Mairet to compose his work on binding.

LORIN, Jean-François *Lyons*

The Lyons Indicateur of 1842 gives him as working at Hôpital 15.

LORTIC *Paris*

According to D. d'E. he started at rue St. Honoré 199 in 1840.

LORY *Paris*

He appears in the 1842–43 Almanachs as working at Chaise 18.

LOUIS *Paris*

At Mont-Hilaire 9 in 1797–98.

LUNIER-BELIER *Paris*

This excellent binder, who exhibited in Paris in the Galeries du Louvre in 1819, dates about 1819–25. I have a specimen of his work in my own collection on the *Poésies de A. de Montesquieu* (two volumes in one) published in 1821. Roth's Cat. No. 9 (1946) shows a full morocco binding by him signed on the spine which appears to be later than my own specimen. On the other hand, Item 223 in Sch. III, hopelessly ill-titled and described, may possibly be rather earlier than my copy.

LUNIERS ? *Paris*

Lesné ('27), p. 290, refers to him with some contempt. He says that he "broche en basane". Probably this means that he "provided cheap and nasty leather covers".

MABILLY, Charles (and stationer) *Marseilles*

Worked between 1841–48 at rue des Templiers 17.

MAILLARD, Alphonse *Bar-le-Duc*

According to D. d'E. worked at rue du Cygne 15 in 1844.

MAILLET, H. *Paris*

Established at Grands-Augustins 20 in 1842, and at No. 27 from 1843–49.

MAILLET-SCHMITZ *Paris*

His addresses seem to have been: Ferme 44 ('42–'47) and Tronchet 15 ('47–'49).

MAILLOT, J. B. *Strassburg*

The 1848 Mercure Alsacien gives his address as Chaudron 9.

MAIRET, François-Ambroise *Dijon*

Was born December 7, 1786. He was first employed by the Court of Appeal, and then became a binder and paper-dealer at rue Rameau, and subsequently from 1819–21 at rue Condé 38. He probably started to bind about 1806, and his chef d'œuvre (see below) was executed in 1812. He left Dijon in 1821, and set up as a paper-manufacturer at Fontenoy, near Montbard. He moved to another paper factory in Brittany about 1830. There is a manuscript biography of him by L. B. Baudot of Dijon, continuing Papillon, Bibliothèque des auteurs de Bourgogne (Dijon, MS. 2063, pp. 1081–2). Long articles regarding him can be found in Thoinan, p. 345, and in Béraldi's *Reliure au XIXe*. He published, among other works, an *Essai sur la reliure et le blanchissement des livres* in 1824, much of which was used by Lenormand and embodied in the Roret Manuels on Binding.
His chef d'œuvre is considered to be the binding on the 3-volume Didot *Racine* of 1801, in blue marbled calf imitating lapis-lazuli and veined

with gold. It was given by the binder to the Dijon Library, where it is still preserved. Other fine examples of his work are described and illustrated in Sch. II, 184/5, Maggs 661/27 and 51, and Béraldi's Reliure pl. 3. Though his talent was much disputed at the time, and his bindings are often inappropriate to the works they cover, he is probably the greatest binder of the time in the use of classical motives, and his work has much charm and delicacy.

MAITRE   *Dijon*

The Dijon Librarian states that he worked for the Library from 1836 when he was at rue du Chapeau-Rouge till 1848, and exhibited in 1837.

MALATI   *Nantes*

Worked in 1808 "près de la Croix-Sainte".

MALET

See Firmin-Didot 1881, No. 410.

MALIBERT

See Bér. V, 298; Romb. 42/3/A.688 and 47/C.542.

MALINVAUD   *Limoges*

At rue Arbre-Peint between 1836–48.

MALLER   *Paris*

At St. Germain-l'Auxerrois 85 from 1847–49.

MAME, *Alfred*   *Tours*

This well-known publisher of moral and educational books started a bindery in 1845.

MANGEZ   *Lille*

Given by the Lille Almanach 1788–89 at rue du Dragon.

MANHES   *Paris*

At Madeleine 51 between 1847–49.

MANNIGEL *Paris*

Worked from 1847–49 at Port-Mahon 5.

MANOEL *Paris*

At Huchette 21 in 1847.

MAQUET *Paris*

The only specimen of this binder, who worked at rue La Paix 26, occurs in Bér. Cat. III, No. 491, as far as my knowledge carries me.

MARANDET *Bordeaux*

At rue Marchande in 1816.

MARCHAND *Bordeaux*

Addresses: rue de Trois-Conils 50 ('19–24); rue de Pergue ('33) rue d'Albret ('36); rue Dufau 15 ('39); 6 ('48).

MARECHAL, *Aîné*

MARESCOT, *fils* *Paris*

Worked at Fosses 14 in 1821.

MARFAN, *Hyppolite* *Bordeaux*

Addresses: rue des Remparts 9 ('39); 73 ('48).

MARFEILLAN *Toulouse*

At Place St. Georges in 1807.

MARGUEREY *Paris*

The Almanachs 1836–49 give his address as Guillemites 2.

MARNAC *Toulouse*

At rue des Paradoux 1833–38.

MAROUF *Lille*

Between 1830–34 at rue du Quai 2.

MAROUFFE   *Lille*

Worked 1841–42 at rue J. J. Rousseau 23.

MARTIN   *Paris*

He appears to have started at St. Jacques 41 in 1797, to have moved to No. 77 in 1809, and finally to Montagne-Ste. Geneviève 52, where he worked between 1834–42.

MARTIN   *Limoges*

At rue Vaubry in 1836.

MARTIN   *Paris*

Worked between 1826–49 as follows: St. Jean-de-Beauvais 24 ('26); St. Honoré 45 ('35); 29 Juillet 6 ('36–'49). My own collection has a fine example of his calf binding with the interesting chrysanthemum border to the sides on Michaud: *Printemps* ('27), and there is an illustrated example of his work in Sch. III, 294.

MARTIN-DELAHAYE   *Lille*

Worked at rue des Arts 28 ('30–'35); No. 50 ('35–'43) as M.-D. Sœurs; and ('44–'45) as Mlle. M.-D.

MARTINAUD, *André*   *Limoges*

Master-binder 1775–89.

MARTINAUD, *Léonard*   *Limoges*

Master-binder 1763–89.

MARTY, *Laurent*   *Toulouse*

At rue Malcousinat in 1838.

MARY, *Ch.*   *Paris*

Worked in 1847 at Passage Bourg-l'Abbé, where his widow is noted in 1849.

MARY & TIREL   *Paris*

At rue des Grands-Augustins 61 in 1834.

MASSE   *Bordeaux*

From 1791–92 at rue du Cahernan.

MASSON (*and gilder*)   *Paris*

His address in 1826 was St. Jean-de-Beauvais 13.

MASSON (*see Capé and Debonnelle*)   *Paris*

MATHIEU   *Limoges*

At rue des Jacobins between 1836–48.

MATHIEU   *Limoges*

Reported at 1848 at rue des Tanneries.

MATHIEU   *Marseilles*

Started in 1813 at rue Haxo; in 1814 went to rue Coutellerie; then in 1818 to Place du Cheval Blanc; and finally to Grand'rue from 1831–38.

MATHIS, A. S.   *Strassburg*

The Mercure Alsacien gives him as at Grand'rue 61 in 1846.

MATHIS, J. J.   *Strassburg*

At Chainé 1 bis in 1846.

MATHIS, Sigismond   *Strassburg*

Worked at Lindenfels 11 in 1824.

MATIFAS   *Paris*

First noted at St. Hilaire 14 in 1816, and later at St. Jean-de-Beauvais 11 from 1826–40.

MATTIFAT   *Paris*

The 1803 Almanach quotes him as working at Montagne 28.

MAUDUIT

137

MAUNIER *Marseilles*

Between 1803–05 at "près des Picpus".

MAURICE *Orleans*

First appears at rue Bretonnière in 1819 and later between 1832–46 at rue Bannier.

MAUSSION *Angers*

At rue St. Laud between 1831–48.

MAYER, *Ed.* *Paris*

Worked at Beaubourg 43 in 1847–49.

MAYNARD *? Paris*

A deaf and dumb binder, a sample of whose work (*c.* 1844) is illustrated in Maggs 661/222. He was possibly a pupil of Lesné, who taught binding at the Deaf and Dumb Institute in Paris towards the end of his life.

MAZARS *Toulouse*

At rue des Gestes in 1807.

MAZEAU *Nantes*

At rue de l'Evêché between 1841–44.

MECHE *Paris*

Between 1847–49 he resided at St. Honoré 297.

MEIGNIE *Paris*

Worked at Perdue 13 from 1832–36.

MEISSIER

MELINET-MALASSIS *Nantes*

At Place Bourbon from 1825–28.

MELLINANT *Montpellier*

Worked at 2 rue St. Charles in 1846 and later at 1 rue St. Pierre.

MELON   *Bordeaux*

   At Place du Palais from 1833–39.

MEMARD   *Paris*

   The 1826 Almanach gives his name at St. Jean-de-Beauvais. Lesné
   notes him as coming to the front about 1820. A binding in my
   possession shows that he was still working in 1837.

MEMER

   Only his name is known to me.

MENARD   *Paris*

   Noted in the 1821 Almanach as at Paon-St. André-des-Arts 8.

MENOU (tools)   *? Paris*

MERCAM   *Bordeaux*

   At rue du Loup 38 between 1836–48.

MERCIER, Christian-Marc   *Paris*

   Thoinan, p. 348, states that he was received in 1777, when he resided
   at Mont-St. Hilaire, and that he makes a last appearance at rue Mignon
   in 1800.

MERCIER   *Paris*

   At Foin-St. Jacques 17 in 1821.

MERCIER   *Paris*

   Worked at Montmartre 26 in 1847.

MERDEL, J. B.   *Strassburg*

   The Mercure Alsacien gives his address in 1846 as Maroquin 12.

MERQUEM

   See Romb. 46/A.605.

MERTZ, F.

His signature appears on a roughly contemporary half-calf binding on Hone's *Every Day Book*, 2 volumes, 1826, in my own collection.

MERVOL

Name noted, without further details.

MESLANT, N. *Paris*

His fortunes seem to have been closely attached to the Orleans family, and in 1836 he styled himself as Binder to the Queen and the Princes and Princesses. According to Thoinan, p. 349, he started at Hillerin-Bertin in 1798. His later addresses were Grenelle 102 (1803); Mathurins 20 ('26); St. Jacques 71 ('43). Lesné speaks rather slightingly of him as a "cartonnier à la Bradel", but he was certainly a first-class binder of wide range. I have an excellent half-morocco binding by him on the first edition of Thiers' *Revolution* 1823, a full morocco binding on two of S. Roger's works executed for Louis Philippe, and a very unusual binding in gilt paper with Leon Gruel's ex-libris. Other illustrations of his work are to be found in Maggs 661/307, Sch. III, 238, and Bér. V, 341. An interesting feature of some of his work is the substitution of black for gold stamping.

Considerable light is thrown on his earlier activities by the entries in the sale catalogues of the Napoleoniana, forming the collection of M. Emile Brouwet, and dispersed at the Salle Drouot in November '34 and May '35. The description of Item 10 in the first sale refers to Meslant as "relieur au Palais" and the illustration reveals a charming binding, unlike anything else I have seen by Meslant. Its probable date might be 1807–08. See also Item 44 in the same catalogue, a binding made for Napoleon and Marie Louise.

MESLIN *Paris*

Noted at Fossés St. Germain 43 between 1847–49.

MESNARD *Paris*

At St. Jacques 112 in 1847 and probably in 1849 when the Almanach gives his name as Memard.

MESPIES *Paris*

Worked in 1842 at Ste. Avoye 52 and Jarente 1.

MESSIER   *Paris*

Appears to have been active at Marais 13 from 1826–42. An example of his work is described in Maggs 661/128 and I have a fine highly gilt calf binding by him (about 1828) formerly in the Béraldi collection.

MESURE   *Limoges*

At rue du Clocher between 1836–48.

MEUNIER   *Paris*

Noted at Viarmes 20 from 1821–26.

MEYER   *Strassburg*

The Mercure Alsacien of 1846 gives his address as Grandes Arcades 39.

MEYNER (*or MEYNIER*)   *Paris*

His addresses were St. Jacques 118 ('21); La Harpe 56 ('26); 64 ('32–'47).

MEYNIEUX   *Limoges*

At rue des Combes in 1848.

MEYNOT & GRESIAUD   *Nantes*

At Place du Pilori 6 between 1841–48.

MICHEL   *Marseilles*

Started in 1812 at rue d'Aubagne 61; at rue Neuve 1 in 1841; rue d'Aubagne 48 in 1844, and No. 59 in 1846.

MICHEL (*and gilder*)   *Paris*

Working at Galande 47 in 1826 and later at No. 45 from 1845–49.

MICHELET   *Paris*

Appears at Sts. Pères 57 from 1842–49.

MICOLCI, (? *Charles*)   *Paris*

The two bindings illustrated in Desc. 437 and Maggs 661/236 cannot be earlier than 1848.

MILARD, *Jean* (*and second-hand books*) *Metz*

Born at Metz and apprenticed in 1777. Worked at Place St. Jacques, and died June 14, 1828, aged 67.

MILARD, *Pierre* *Metz*

Son of the above, continued to bind till his death on January 25, 1871.

MILLET *Paris*

First appears in 1832 at Neuve-St. Roch, then at Galande 47 ('36), and finally at Thérèse 4 ('42–'47).

MINOST

Again only his name is known.

MITRAUD *Bordeaux*

At rue des Trois-Conils 35 in 1848.

MOINARD *Bordeaux*

At rue du Château-Trompette ('16); rue Porte-Dijeaux 24 ('19–'24).

MONIER, (*Tools*) *? Paris*

Mentioned by Lesné ('27), p. 305, as the "athlete" who had replaced Culembourg and Kilcher as tool cutters.

MONLON *Paris*

Worked at Anglais 9 from 1842–49.

MONNIER *Paris*

At Charretière 9 in 1809.

MONNIOT, *Louis* *Lyons*

He is mentioned in the 1832 Lyons Indicateur without address, and in 1842 as at Thomassin 27. My own collection contains a probably contemporary binding on a Manuale dated 1835.

MONSACRE *Bordeaux*

At rue St. Dominique, à l'Académie, in 1836–48.

MONSELLE   *Paris*

   Worked at Amandiers 13 between 1842–43.

MONTAGNE   *Paris*

   First noted in 1842 at St. Jean-de-Beauvais 13, and then at Noyers 52
   between '47 and '49.

MONTHEROT

   Reported by D. d'E. as working in 1829.

MORAIN   *Paris*

   The 1840–43 Almanachs give his address as Faubourg St. Martin 43.

MOREAU   *Paris*

   Working at Parcheminerie 2 in 1842.

MORET   *Paris*

   The Almanachs between 1832–49 give his address as St. Jacques 110.

MORIGNE (*Morinier*)   *Angers*

   At Chaussée St. Père between 1831–48.

MORTIER   *Bordeaux*

   At rue Devise-Ste. Cathérine 20 in 1839.

MOSSNER

   No particulars are available.

MOTET   *Paris*

   The Sch. Cat. II, 157–8 describes and illustrates two rather dull
   signed bindings of the transition period, probably about 1798–1800,
   and Mr. J. F. Smith, of the City of Liverpool Public Libraries, reports
   his signature on a Paris publication dated 1809. The only reference
   to him in the Almanachs is in 1821, when his address was Sorbonne 12.

MOTRIEU   *Paris*

   His address was Trévise 9 from 1842–49.

MOTTE, A.

See Bér. III, 106.

MOUILLIE   *Paris*

He appears in the 1797 Almanach at St. Jacques 55, and Thoinan quotes him as working in 1803. He appears to have also worked at Nos. 69 and 65 of the same street. Examples of his work appear in Sch. II, 128–32, and in my own collection. A poor binder, with little or no originality, so far as I have seen his work.

MOUREAU   *Marseilles*

Started at rue Vieux-St. Ferréol in 1803, then at rue Maucouinat ('05); rue d'Aubagne 9 ('12) and 26 ('18–'28).

MOURON, *Claude*   *Lyons*

According to Gruel I, p. 148, this apprentice-binder was executed in 1793. His address was rue des Fouettés.

MOUSSET-THOUVENIN   *Paris*

Worked at Boulevard du Temple 4 in 1847.

MOUTAILLIER   *Paris*

The 1842 Almanach mentions him at Poupée 5.

MUHLBERGER, E.   *Strassburg*

Given in the Mercure Alsacien of 1846 as at Cordonniers 3.

MULLER, R. *and/or* F.   *Paris*

It is almost as difficult to follow this binder (or binders) as to trace the Herings. My own impression is that the important Muller was "R", and that "F" was a less important brother or cousin. The only two appearances of a Muller in the Almanachs between 1820–40 appear to be: (1) "J. Hering and F. Muller" in 1832 at Coquenard 24; and (2) Muller at the same address in 1835. This "F" Muller seems hardly likely to have been the same as the Muller who signs "R. Muller, Succr. Thouvenin" about 1834 (the year of Thouvenin's death), and later, up to his own death in 1836, as "Muller" tout court.

The Muller seems to have worked with Hering between 1821–26 (and even again about 1834) and then possibly about 1826 joined Thouvenin, who states that it was only by about 1830 that he was able to build up a really competent team of binders. My own collection contains an excellent binding signed "R. Muller, Succr. Thouvenin", using a well-known Thouvenin tool on the back, and a charming purple-stamped velvet binding, similarly signed, on Daniell's *India*, with the well-known seated woman's figure, for which also see Bér. Rel., pl. 58.

MULLER   *Paris*

Appears at Passage Dauphine in 1842.

MULLER, Veuve.   *Paris*

MUNET   *Paris*

According to the 1832 Almanach he was then working at St. Jacques 77.

MUNIER   *Paris*

Worked at various addresses between 1815–49, as follows: Place Cambrai 8 ('15); St. Jacques 77 ('21); No. 63 ('36); Ecole de Médecine 34 ('47); Sorbonne 4 ('49).

MURIE   *Paris*

After working at Bourbon-Villeneuve 8 in 1838, he moved two years later to Cherche-Midi 8.

MUSSEL, Georges-Frederic   *Strassburg*

The Strohl Manuel of 1824 gives his address as l'Hôpital 33.

MUSSEL, Philippe-Jacques   *Strassburg*

The same Manuel for 1824 refers to this second Müssel as at l'Hôpital 25.

MUZATON   *Paris*

Working at Sentier 26 between 1836–43.

NAIL   *Angers*

At rue St. Gilles between 1831–40.

NAISSANT   *Paris*

He first appears at Sept-Voies 31 in 1803, and finally at No. 8 in 1821. Lesné ('27), p. 107, refers to his talent for binding church books for the lectern.

NAISSANT, Fils   *Paris*

Mentioned in 1826 as at Montagne-Ste. Geneviève 15.

NANCEY, F.

No details available.

NARCY (see PENNEL-NARCY)   *Lille*

At rue de Tournay 60 in 1835.

NEISSE   *Paris*

The 1837 Almanach gives his address as Poissonière 36.

NEREAUDEAU   *Paris*

He figures in the 1842–47 Almanachs at Fossés-Montmartre 16–18. Under the first date he is described as the successor of Villemsons, importers of English bindings.

NESBOM   *Paris*

At St. André-des-Arts 41 in 1816. Lesné '27, pp. 327 and 335, refers to him obscurely but unflatteringly as Nesbons and Nebons.

NESSEAUT   *Paris*

Almanach Typographique 1799 gives him at rue Sept-Voies.

NICOLAS, Jacques   *Lyons*

The 1821 Lyons Indicateur locates him at rue Royale 12.

NICOLET   *? Paris*

Mentioned by Lesné '27, p. 377, as one of the best edge-marblers.

NIEDREE (*Niedrée et Cie.*)   *Paris*

He was born at Saarbruck in 1803 and died about 1856. One of the best pupils of Thouvenin, he succeeded Muller on the latter's death in 1836 as "successor to Thouvenin", when he styled himself "Ancienne Maison Thouvenin". His addresses appear to have been Passage Dauphine 7 and Mazarine 29 (see Almanachs 1840–47).

NIODOT   *Paris*

Appears in 1821 at Fossés 14.

NIQUET (*and gilder*)   *Paris*

Addresses: Gravilliers 22 ('35); Temple 37 ('38); Chaillot 42 ('42); Lancry 25 ('47).

NOE   *Paris*

The 1842 Almanach mentions him as at Mail 18.

NOEL   *? Besançon*

Examples of his work are illustrated in Sch. III, 224–5, and I have a specimen in my own collection which bears out Lesné '27, p. 90, that he was stingy with his gold. He worked about 1803–05, and possibly considerably later, as Lesné evidently regarded him as a contemporary about 1820.

NOEL, F.   *Paris*

The 1821–43 Almanachs give his address at Pierre-Sarrasin 3.

NOEL, *Jeune (and gilder)*   *Paris*

Practised at various addresses as follows: St. Jacques 27 ('21); La Harpe 58 ('26); Montagne-Ste. Geneviève 52 ('36–'43).

NOLOT   *Paris*

At Plâtre St. Jacques 24 in 1832.

NOUBEL, *Veuve et Fils*   *Agen*

The binding illustrated in Sch. II, 113, on *La Constitution Française*, though falling within the dates of this study, is completely eighteenth century. The binder's address is given as rue Garonne, and the prices for different styles of binding are quoted.

NOUHAUD   *Limoges*

At rue Petites-Pousses between 1836–48.

NOUVEL   *Paris*

Worked at Plâtre St. Jacques 11 between 1842–49.

NUTZBAUM

The only information which I have regarding this binder is contained in the description and illustration of Sch. III, 312.

OBERMANN

See Bér. V, 311.

OBRE (*gatherer and sewer*)   *Paris*

Working in 1815–16 at Noyers 25.

OGEZ   *Paris*

First noted in 1815 at St. Jacques 124, and finally at No. 27 in 1821.

OGINSKI, Prince G.   *Paris*

Thoinan, p. 226, footnote refers to this Polish exile as having set up a binding business staffed by his fellow-exiles at Barrière du Roule about 1835. Cat. 18 of A. Rosenthal Ltd., Oxford, Nos. 225 and 227 records two specimens of his work.

ORLIAC   *Moissac*

Romb. 47/c. 554 records a cartonnage of the period by the above on Vigny's *Poèmes*, 2nd edition, 1829.

ORLOWSKI   *Paris*

Though mentioned in the 1849 Almanach as at Parcheminerie 2, he must be regarded, in default of evidence to the contrary, as outside our period.

ORY

I have only a note that he may have been binding about 1822.

OTTMANN (I)   *Paris*

His daughter married Duplanil **Fils**. He probably worked between 1825–40. A specimen of his work is illustrated in Bér. Cat. V, 235, and my own collection contains a calf binding with effective straight line work.

OTTMANN (II)   *Paris*

OTTMANN-DUPLANIL   *Paris*

His addresses were: Four 67 ('40); No. 37 ('43); Cherche-Midi 19 ('49). An example of his work is illustrated in Desc. II, 317.

OTTO, A.   *Boulogne*

The Boulogne Annuaire of 1848 gives his address as Carreaux 48. In mid-1949 I noted a very high-class binding by him (slightly earlier than 1848) in M. Van der Parre's shop in Brussels.

OUDOT   *Paris*

Was working at St. Jean-de-Beauvais 31 in 1803.

PAGET   *Bordeaux*

At rue du Cahernan 5 between 1805–24.

PAILLET   *Orleans*

First noted in 1814 at Place du Marché au Pain, and then in 1819 at rue Royale.

PALYART, F.   *Paris*

In 1847 he was domiciled at Poissonière 5.

PAMPIN, Michel   *Lyons*

His addresses, all in the Grande rue Mercière, were as follows: No. 45 ('10); No. 61 ('13); No. 44 ('21).

PAQUET, Etienne   *Lyons*

From 1810–21 he worked at Raisin 7.

PAQUET, P. *Paris*

The Almanachs note him at Carmes 5 in 1815, and at Bièvre 13 in 1826. Bér. Cat. III, No. 439, is the only specimen known to me.

PARADIS *Paris*

Was at Amandiers 6 in 1803.

PARVY *Limoges*

At rue-Neuve-des-Charseix in 1848.

PASTRE *St. Omer*

I have no further information.

PAULIN

Signed the binding of an 1840 keepsake (see Cat. Deglatigny No. 116). (See also Romb. '42–'43 A.707.)

PAULINIER *Paris*

Noted in 1821 as at Sèvres 4.

PAULMIER *Dunkirk*

Was at rue du Moulin in 1788, and probably, from an undated Almanach, later at rue des Prêtres, having possibly succeeded Archange (q.v.).

PECLET *Paris*

Appears from 1847–49 at Hauteville 7.

PEIFFER (*and music-ruler*) *Paris*

His address was Place Royale 18. I have seen a full morocco album with his signed label dated 1810 on a collection of airs, etc., at Rossignol's shop, May 1949.

PELICIER (*and gilder*) *Paris*

After five years from 1816 at Dauphine 35, he went to Place St. André-des-Arts 7 in 1821, where he stayed till 1838. Lesné '27, p. 190, refers to him as the supreme fore-edge gilder of his day.

PLATE II   A. de Beauvais

PELLERIN, *Jean Baptiste (and images)* *Metz*

Born at Epinal September 11, 1787. Worked at rue de Ponteffroy and then at rue des Jardins. Died March 10, 1841.

PELLERIN, *Adolphe* *Metz*

Son of the above. Born July 1, 1827. Worked at rue St. Médard 1 c. Left Metz in 1871.

PELLETIER, P.

Sch. III, 237, illustrates a probably contemporary binding on an 1811 Racine.

PENET *Lyons*

The Lyons Indicateur mentions him in 1832.

PENNEL-NARCY (*see* NARCY) *Lille*

At rue St. Jacques 16 ('41); Place de la Mairie 16 ('43–'48).

PERE *Paris*

Worked at Deux Portes-St. Sauveur 16 in 1843.

PERREAU

Romb. 47/G. 76 refers to a half-calf contemporary binding by Perreau, *c.* 1828.

PERRIE *Bayonne*

Was at rue des Basques 33 about 1840–50.

PERRIER

Only his name is known to me.

PERRIN, *Louis-Antoine* *Paris*

Received 1773, and lived at rue des Carmes. In 1798 he was at St. Jacques 70, and later at Nos. 667 ('03); 77 ('09); and 70 ('15). (See Thoinan, p. 371.)

PLATE III   Béraud, Aîné

153

PERRIN   *Paris*

At Huchette 6–8 in 1816. May have been the same as the above though Perrin Fils was at St. Jacques 70 in 1816.

PERRIN, *Fils*   *Paris*

Probably the son of Louis-Antoine, and noted as at L.A.'s address (St. Jacques 70) in 1816.

PERRIN, *Jeune*   *Paris*

Working at Lune 37 in 1826.

PERSIN   *Paris*

According to the Almanachs his addresses were as follows: Galande 51 ('21); Harpe 40 ('26); Noyers 34 ('32–'47).

PERTUISOT   *Paris*

According to A. M-S, p. 361, he was binder to "La Cour des Comptes". His addresses were: Théâtre Français ('99); Liberté 68 ('03); Odéon 38 ('15); St. Jacques 39 ('21–'26).

PESEUX   *Paris*

First at Dragon 8 in 1836, and then at No. 20 from 1838–49.

PESEUX   *Paris*

Worked at St. Marc 22 in 1842 and at No. 20 in 1847.

PETAIL   *Orleans*

Was at rue Ste. Cathérine in 1846.

PETER, *A.*   *Strassburg*

The Mercure Alsacien gives his address in 1846 as Veaux 24.

PETIT   *Paris*

See Thoinan, p. 372. Addresses: St. Jacques 644 (1797); Folies-Monsieur-le-Prince (1799); St. Jacques 110 (1800–21).

PETIT, *Charles*   *Paris*

Noted 1843–49 at Faubourg du Roule 15.

PLATE IV   Ch. Blaise

PETIT-GUYOT, *Pierre-François* *Lyons*

His address in 1832 was Thomassin 2.

PETITOT *Lille*

Given in the 1788–89 Almanach as at rue Neuve. Between 1829–48 there was a Petitot at No. 37 in the same street.

PEYROL *Paris*

At Taitbout 36 from 1842–47.

PEZIEUX, *A-LESPINASSE* *Paris*

Given in the 1840 Almanach at St. Martin 102.

PFANNMULLER *Paris*

Appears as a binder and gilder at Seine 9 under date of 1843.

PFEHFEL *Paris*

This binder and gilder figures in 1842 at Four-St. Germain 7 (possibly the same as Pfeiffer, *q.v.*).

PFEIFFER *Paris*

Worked between 1834–49 at Four-St. Germain 7. I have a 2 volume Grandville: *Animaux* 1842 in a typical rather heavy gilt morocco binding.

PFISTER *Paris*

At Harpe 98 between 1847–49.

PFLUGER *Strassburg*

The Mercure Alsacien of 1846 mentions him at Grande rue de l'Eglise 9.

PICARD, (? *Noël*) *Paris*

Lesné ('27) mentions him on p. 350 as small fry. His address in 1821 was Mail 8.

PLATE V Cassassus

157

PICON (PICHON)   *Marseilles*

    At Ste. Marthe 1 ('24); rue du Beausset ('27–'38); and rue des Beaux-Arts 3 in 1848.

PIED, *Antoine*   *Paris*

    He is referred to by Thoinan, p. 373, and in the 1803–21 Almanachs. His addresses were: Sept-Voies in 1776 when he was received; Place Cambrai ('99); Anglais ('99); St. Jean-de-Beauvais 14 ('03); Mathurins 24 ('09 onwards).

PIERRE   *Paris*

    At St. Etienne-Bonne Nouvelle 5 from 1842–47.

PIERRY, *Mme. (edge-gilder)*   *Paris*

    Styles herself as the successor of Longre, of whom nothing appears to be known. Her address in 1835 was St. Honoré 58, and from 1838–42 she was at Tirechappe 16.

PILLET   *Paris*

    His address in 1842 is given as St. Jean-de-Beauvais 11.

PIRON   *Sablé*

    According to a note received from M. Paul Cordonnier, he was working at Sablé in 1844.

PITON, *Ch.*   *Strassburg*

    From the address ascribed to him in 1846 by the Mercure Alsacien he may have succeeded Jean-Philippe Piton.

PITON, *Frédéric*   *Strassburg*

    The Strohl Manuel 1824 gives his address as Salzman 6, and the 1846 Mercure Alsacien as Juifs 8 (initial "F" only). The binding illustrated and described in Sch. III, 301, is a facsimile of one in my own collection. Many of the tools approximate so closely to those used by Thraner, that he must at least have been his pupil.

PITON, *Jean-Philippe*   *Strassburg*

    His address in 1824 was Place du Temple-Neuf 15.

PLATE VI Comte de Caumont

159

PLANY   *Paris*

Worked at Cul-de-Sac des Bœufs in 1803.

PLATIAUX   *Lille*

At rue d'Amiens 8 in 1835–37.

PLESSIER   *Nantes*

Addresses: rue Crébillon ('17); rue du Calvaire 23 ('41); rue de l'Ecluse
4 ('44–'45).

PLUMET   *Paris*

See Thoinan, p. 378 and Almanachs 1797–1809. Worked at Quai
Conti 1881, which in 1808 became Quai de la Monnaie 21.

POCHET   *Orleans*

Worked at rue d'Illiers between 1814–46.

POCHET, Fils   *Orleans*

Noted at rue Vieille Foulerie in 1846.

POLIAC   *Paris*

Lived at Mail 33 from 1832–35.

POLIET

His signature (*c.* 1840) is reported by D. d'E.

POLLANE   *Angers*

At rue Chaperonnière between 1831–48.

POMMEREAU   *Paris*

First noted at Sept-Voies 35 in 1835; then at Cluny 1 and Place
Sorbonne 1 in 1842–49.

PONCEL, V. T.

No details available.

PLATE VII   I. Deforge

161

PONGE

I have a half-calf binding signed by him, evidently dating about 1825.

PONTHIER   *Bordeaux*

Addresses: rue du Loup ('91–'92); rue Trois-Conils 46 ('07–'11); rue du Cahernan 39 ('16–'19); rue des Ayres ('24).

PONTIER, *Citoyenne*   *Paris*

Thoinan, p. 379, mentions her as working at rue de la Harpe 1799–1800.

PONTIER   *Paris*

He worked at St. Jean-de-Beauvais 11 from 1815–38.

PONTIER, *Fils*   *Paris*

First noted at Amandiers 15 in 1836, then at St. Jean-de-Beauvais 20 in ('38), and finally at No. 11 in ('42).

POREY, *Ch.*

The binding illustrated and described in Sch. III, 288, is not earlier in date than 1821, and from its appearance may well be provincial.

PORISE   *Lille*

At rue Neuve ('35); and at rue du Tenremonde 32 ('38–'48).

POSTIAU-DUFEY   *Lille*

Worked from 1829–44 at Quai de la Basse-Deûle 5.

POTHEY *or* POTHE   *Dijon*

See *Pottié.*

POTHIER *or* POTTIER, *Jacques*   *Paris*

Received in 1774, and resided at rue d'Ecosse; later, in 1798, at Quai Conti (see Thoinan, p. 380).

POTIER, *C.-O.*   *Paris*

Was at Hautefeuille 20 from 1840–42.

PLATE VIII   Desmais

163

POTIN   *Nantes*

> At rue Bertrand-Molleville 10 in 1828.

POTTIE   *Dijon*

> A report dated August 16, 1821 by the Dijon Librarian states that
> he had divided an award for binding between the above, Lorillard,
> Pralon, and Jacotier, who had each offered specimens of their work
> to the town. He is also mentioned as Pothey and Pothé between
> 1818–27.

POUGNY   *Paris*

> A gilder, said to have been one of the elder Simier's main props.

PRALON, *Hubert*   *Dijon*

> This pupil of Mairet was born at Dijon on July 30, 1797, and died
> at Vannerie 69 in 1871. His only other known address is Chaudron-
> nerie 27 in 1832. He was succeeded by his son Claude, and then by
> his grandson. All the family worked for the Dijon Library. His early
> bindings, as typified by a marbled calf specimen in my own collection
> dating about 1821, are in the direct Mairet tradition, and show many
> of Mairet's usual tools. Later bindings, as shown in Sch. III, 313,
> are typical of the period, but indicate that he had abandoned the
> classical "motifs" of his distinguished master.

PREMIER, *Pierre*   *Lyons*

> The Lyons Indicateur of 1842 gives his address as Tupin 16.

PREVOST   *Paris*

> The 1842–49 Almanachs note him as working at Marais St. Germain
> 13.

PREVOST *or* PREVOT   *Paris*

> Worked at Amandiers 17 from 1797–1815, when he transferred to
> No. 10.

PRIEZ   *Paris*

> He is mentioned in the 1799 and 1803 Almanachs at Mont-St. Hilaire
> 10.

PLATE IX   Dupin, Fils

165

PRINCE   *Paris*

At Dragon 4 in 1847.

PRODEL, P.

Signature on original edition of St. Beuve's *Volupté*, (Blaizot, February 1950.)

PRUDON   *Dôle*

He showed at the Arts Exhibition at Dijon in 1837.

PRUDHOMME, *Mathieu*   *Lyons*

The 1842 Lyons Indicateur gives his address at Galerie de l'Argus.

PRUNET   *Toulouse*

At rue St. Sernin in 1807.

PRUNET   *Toulouse*

At rue des Arts ('38); rue du Musée 7 ('47–'48).

PRUNIER   *Paris*

Worked at Zacharie 9 from 1842–49.

PRUNIER   *Paris*

Appears at St. Séverin 16 in 1847–49.

PUJO   *Paris*

The 1832–47 Almanachs give his address as Neuve-St. Roch 23.

PUJOS   *Bordeaux*

Addresses: rue St. Dominique 1 ('19–'22); rue Porte-Dijeaux 78 ('33); rue des Remparts ('36).

PURGOLD, L. G.   *Paris*

Little seems to be known of this great figure in romantic binding, who died in his heyday in 1830. He is first mentioned in the Almanachs in 1816 at Dauphine 35; received a Medal of Honour in 1819; moved to Cassette 18 in ('21); and apparently after 1826 to rue du Roule 15.

PLATE X Gaudreau

167

My own collection contains specimens of his more elaborate binding on eight volumes of Volney's *Œuvres* ('21), with the Coventry arms and rich spines, borders, and silk end-papers, and of his simplest binding, in which the straight line, which he was to hand on to Bauzonnet, predominates with amazing effect. I have seen a binding exactly similar to the above at Blaizot's signed Bauzonnet-Purgold. By 1829 he was signing both as "Purgold" and as "Bauzonnet-Purgold". His artistic place is dealt with in the introduction to this work.

PURGOLD and HERING   *Paris*

There seems to be no way of dating exactly these combinations in which Purgold, Hering, and Muller played their part, but this may have been one of the earliest. The example in my own collection is an elaborate Italianate morocco binding on Clisson's *Voyage Pittoresque*, dated 1817, and I should be inclined to date it four to six years later.

QUANNONE   *Paris*

Operated at various addresses as follows: Carmes 28 ('35); Argenteuil 52 ('40); St. Honoré 276 ('43); Mt. Thabor 28 ('49).

QUARTEAU   *? Paris*

Lesné '27, p. 214, mentions him as a good gilder on leather.

QUAU   *Orleans*

At rue Bourgogne in 1814–19.

QUAU, *Veuve*   *Orleans*

Had succeeded her husband by 1832.

QUESNAY   *Paris*

The 1835 Almanach places him at St. Jean-de-Beauvais 28.

QUICHERAT   *Paris*

At Vieille-du-Temple 92 in 1842.

PLATE XI   Guerrinot

169

QUINET								*Paris*

His address, 1847–49, was Bussy 15.

QUINQUEMPOIX							*Doullens*

He appears to have combined a bookselling and binding business
at rue du Bourg in 1827.

RABIER								*Nantes*

Addresses: Passage du Commerce ('04); rue Rameau ('08); Barillerie
('17); Basse Grande-rue ('30–'48).

RACI								*Versailles*

Lived at rue Dauphine. Bound for Marie-Antoinette till 1788 (see
Gruel II, p. 134). There is no proof that he bound later.

RAVARD								*Nantes*

Addresses: Haute Grande-rue ('41); Place St. Jean 4 ('43); Place de
la Commune ('45).

RAYGER, *Daniel*							*Strassburg*

The Strohl Manuel of 1824 gives his address as Epine 6.

RAYMOND								*Limoges*

Worked at Faubourg Manigne in 1848.

REDON								*Paris*

Thoinan, p. 383, gives his address as St. Jean-de-Beauvais in 1799,
and Salle Neuve du Palais 1800–02.

REDON								*Paris*

Thoinan, p. 383, places him at rue Colombier in 1799 and at Quai
Voltaire in 1802–03.

REDON, *Jean and Louis*						*Paris*

Both figure in the Valade Almanach for 1789 but Thoinan, p. 382,
holds that the latter died in that year.

PLATE XII   J. Hering

171

REDSLOB   *Strassburg*

    Worked at Sanglier 13 in 1824.

REDSLOB, *Daniel-Frédéric*   *Strassburg*

    Noted in 1824 at Maroquin 23.

REGNARD   *Paris*

    First noticed at Guisarde 19 in 1839, and between 1840–42 at St. Benoît 8 bis.

REICHMANN   *Paris*

    The 1842–49 Almanachs quote him at St. Benoit 19, with a note that he had received a "B" mention in 1839. There seems some doubt as to whether he was more than a maker of temporary holders.

REITZ (*see Vernier*)

REMIOT   *Paris*

    At Arbre-Sec 6 in 1839.

REMY, H.   *Paris*

    Worked 1847–49 at St. Louis-Marais 23/25.

RENAULT   *Paris*

    The 1809 Almanach mentions him at Gît-le-Cœur 8.

RENAUD (*or RENAUX*)   *Lille*

    At rue de Roubaix 5 ('38); rue des Fossés 40 ('48).

REQUIEM   *Paris*

    His address in 1835 was Bertin-Poirée 2.

REUILLIR   *Lille*

    Cour du Pourpoint d'Or 3 in 1846–48.

REVEL   *Toulouse*

    At rue Fourbastard 12 in 1847–48.

PLATE XIII   Jacotier

REVERSAT   *Montpellier*

Worked at rue du Palais between 1843–45.

REY   *Paris*

Lived at St. Honoré 163 in 1832 and then at Place-St. Michel 8 in 1835–36.

REY, *Mathieu*   *Marseilles*

Started at Maucouinat 25 in 1845 and was at rue d'Aubagne 48 between 1846–48.

REY   *Toulouse*

Addresses: rue Pargaminières 74 ('38); petite rue Ste. Ursule ('48).

RHEIN, G.   *Strassburg*

Given in the 1846 Mercure Alsacien as at Grand' rue 143.

RIBOLET   *Paris*

Worked at Visitation des Dames 10 from 1843–47.

RICARD   *Douai*

Appears in the 1788 Almanach as at rue des Procureurs.

RICHARD   *Paris*

Practised at Dauphine 41 in 1842–49.

RICHARD, *Victor*   *Paris*

The 1842–49 Almanachs give his address as St. Honoré 89.

RIEHL, *Jean-Jacques*   *Strassburg*

The Strohl Manuel mentions him in 1842 at Petites Boutiques 35.

RIGE   *Paris*

His addresses were as follows: Carmes 23 ('32); St. Hilaire 14 ('36); St. Jean-de-Beauvais 20 ('47–'49).

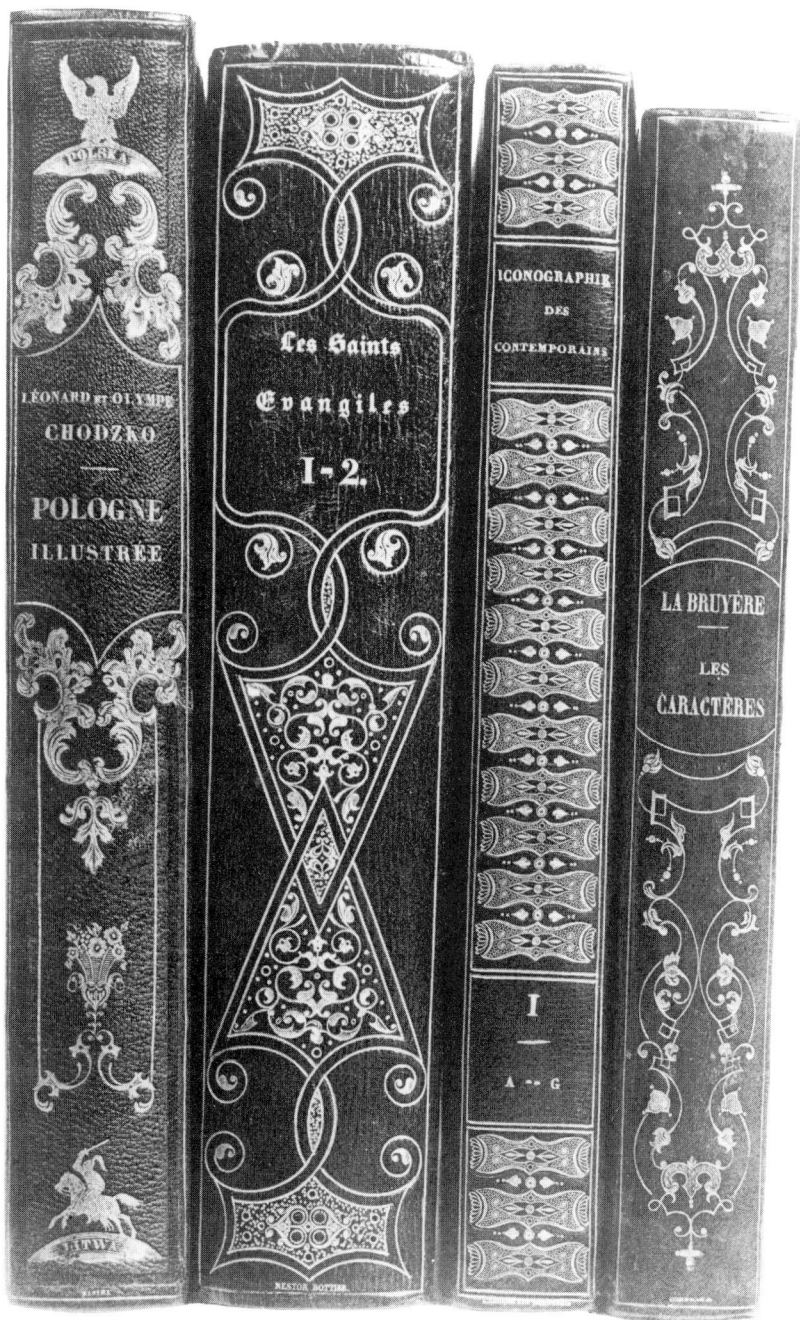

PLATE XIV   Kisiel: Nestor Bottier:
R. Muller. succ. Thouvenin: J. Corfmat

RINOIS

Only his name is known to me.

RISCE

Rombaldi '47/A.689, refers to a contemporary binding by the above on *Le Camélia*, 1839.

RISS *et SAUCET*   *Moscow*

An example of these binders' work is described and illustrated in Sch. IV, 74. From the label and general style of the work, there is little doubt as to the French origin of the binders. The binding dates about 1797.

RIVAGE   *Paris*

He is first noted in 1838 at St. Jacques 104, and then at Sorbonne 4 in 1842–43. The rocaille binding in my own collection may be slightly later in date.

ROBERT   *Limoges*

At rue Fourie in 1848.

ROBERT   *Paris*

I have only been able to trace him in 1842 at St. Martin 138, though R.L.B. states that he was working as early as 1836.

ROBERTJAU (-*JOT or* -*GEAU*)   *Nantes*

Addresses: Fenelon 4 ('04); à la Halte, à la Bibliothèque de la Ville ('08); Thurot ('17–'18).

ROBY, *Jean*   *Limoges*

Master-binder in 1789. Limoges records carry him as far back as the incredible date of 1705.

ROCHE, *Maturin*   *Limoges*

Master-binder in 1789.

PLATE XV Kleinhans

177

ROCHE, *Jeune*   *Limoges*

At rue du Clocher in 1836. There are two very simple bindings signed "Roche" in the Limoges Library.

ROESER

Romb. '47/A. 671, refers to an elaborate binding by the above, but gives no indication of its date or nationality, beyond the date of the work in question, which is 1813.

ROINI   *Paris*

The Almanach Typographique of 1799 reports him at rue des Amandiers (? see Leroyny).

ROMAGNESI, *Charles*   *Paris*

Worked at a variety of addresses as follows: St. Jacques 105 ('32); Noyers 32 ('36); Harpe 58 ('40); Plâtre-St. Jacques 58 ('42); 15 ('42–'49).

RONDEAU   *? Paris*

This binder is only known to me by a luxurious binding (own collection) in the Tessier style on Coffinière's *Décisions sur le Code Napoléon*, 1809. Cambacérès' arms figure on the sides and this was evidently the author's dedication copy to him.

ROOS   *Paris*

Figures at Faubourg-St. Antoine 59 in 1847–49.

ROOS, *Philippe-Jacques*   *Strassburg*

First mentioned in the Strohl Manuel in 1824, and probably the same as the Ph. Roos in the 1846 Mercure Alsacien.

ROSA   *Paris*

He was a well-known publisher of calendars, almanachs, and other small gift books, as well as a binder. He appears in the 1809 Almanach and I have a charming binding by him at least a year later. His work can be seen in Maggs 661/17, and Sch. III, 215/7. His address was Bussy 15, and I suspect that he may have been working as early as 1791.

PLATE XVI Lacouture

179

ROSSIGNOL   *Paris*

Noted at Quai des Orfèvres 4 in 1843.

ROSSIGNOL, *Veuve*   *Paris*

Worked between 1832 and 1838 at St. Dominique 13.

ROUGIER (*or* ROUZIER)   *Limoges*

Addresses: rue des Combes ('36); rue Vigenaud ('46); rue de la
Comédie ('48).

ROULLIN   *Paris*

His addresses were: Ste. Barbe 4 ('32); No. 8 ('35); Bergère 24 ('47);
No. 30 ('49).

ROUSSEAU   *Paris*

Noted at Quincampoix 8 in 1843. He apparently did binding on
commission for booksellers.

ROUSELLE   *Lille*

At Cour d'Assonville 17 ('47); rue des Fives 2 ('48).

ROUSSELOT, *André Hippolyte*   *Metz*

Born at Metz August 1, 1821. First did binding which he left for
bookselling in 1854. Died January 1, 1884.

ROUSSET   *Paris*

Worked at Place Cambrai 3 from 1815–26. Lesné '27, p. 214, classes
him as a gilder, and supreme in his line, though in the Almanachs
he is listed as a binder, without any reference to his being a gilder.

ROUSSET, *Père*   *Paris*

The 1832 Almanach gives his address as St. Jacques 105.

ROYER (*or* ROYE), H.   *Bordeaux*

There are for this binder some variations of name and addresses.
The following are those known to me: Royer, rue du Loup (1789–92);
Royé, H., rue du Loup 20 (1807–11); Royer, Père et Fils, rue du Loup

PLATE XVII   A. L'Anglois

20 ('16–'19); Royer, same address ('24); rue du Chateau Royal ('33–'36) Place Tourny 1 ('39); *Père*, Place Tourny 2 ('48); *Fils*, rue Condillac 1 ('48).

ROYER & DESPIERRES   *Bordeaux*

In 1839 at rue Ste. Cathérine 58.

RUAU, *Aîné*   *Paris*

Worked at various numbers in St. Jean-de-Beauvais as follows: 13 ('32); 20 ('40); 11 ('47–'49).

RUAU, *Jeune*   *Paris*

Noted at St. Jean-de-Beauvais 13 in 1842.

RUAUD   *Limoges*

At Boulevard du Collège ('36); Faubourg Boucherie ('46–'48).

RUPRECHT   *Paris*

Appears in the 1826 Almanach at Petit-Lion 11.

SABOT, *Geoffroi-Marie*   *Paris*

From information gathered from Thoinan, p. 390, and from the Almanachs, it appears that he was received in 1778, and lived in St. Jean-de-Beauvais. About 1800 he moved to Gît-le-Cœur 18, and in 1809–10 he lived at No. 4 in the same street.

SAGE   *Paris*

His address in 1838 was Hôtel-Colbert 16, and in 1842 St. Jacques 110.

SAGE, *Bertrand* (*Aîné en* 1838)   *Toulouse*

Addresses: rue des Cordeliers ('07); rue du Taur ('33–'38).

SAGE, *Jacques*   *Toulouse*

At rue du Collège ('38); rue Pargaminières ('47–'48).

SAGE   *Toulouse*

His address in 1839–48 was rue des Lois.

PLATE XVIII   Larrivière

SAINT-HUBERT   *Bordeaux*

   At rue des Religieuses 23 in 1836.

ST. RIQUIER   *Paris*

   His activities seem to have been centred in Rue St. Jacques as follows:
   No. 27 ('38); 39 ('40); 59 ('43).

SALEL, H.

   My own collection contains a typical calf binding with blind-stamped
   sides on the 2 volume Scarron: *Roman Comique*, published by Mars
   in 1825.

SALEL, R.

   A binding signed by this binder was seen at the shop of G. Salet,
   Paris, in February 1950.

SAMFIN, Jean-Louis   *Paris*

   Received in 1776, and lived at rue des Carmes. Probably moved to
   rue St. Jacques in 1800, was at No. 627 in ('03) and at 124 from 1809–
   16. (See Thoinan, p. 390.)

SAMUEL, A.   *Strassburg*

   At Petites Boucheries 108 in 1846.

SANIER, Veuve   *Paris*

   Appears in 1803 at Carmes 6.

SAR(R)AZIN, Pierre-François   *Paris*

   Received in 1777, lived at rue Judas, and moved to rue Mathurins
   in 1800 (Thoinan, p. 390). In 1803 he was at Mathurins 329, and at
   No. 20 in 1809–16. In the 1815 Almanach he is styled Sarazin *Père*.

SARAZIN   *Cahors*

   In July 1949, M. Léon Gruel informed me of the existence of this
   binder, without any dates as to his activity.

PLATE XIX   Lebatteux

SARAZIN, Fils   *Paris*

Worked at St. Jacques 95 in 1815; at Mathurins 20 in 1821, and from 1826–47 at No. 140. In 1838 he dropped the "Fils".

SARDIS   *Athens*

Quoted to me by M. Léon Gruel as a French binder of the epoch.

SAUINIER

Romb. 46/A.603 mentions a contemporary binding on a work dated 1846.

SAUTELET

May have been working about 1845.

SAUVAGE, Louis   *Paris*

Married the daughter of P. L. Lefèbvre, who received her father's business as dower. He lived at rue des Amandiers and is known to have worked between 1786–89. (See Thoinan, p. 327.)

SAYET   *? Paris*

Lesné '27, pp. 77 and 123, refers to him as the supreme marbler of end-papers, and as having lost his eyesight from the acids which he employed in the process.

SCHAECK   *Paris*

He is quoted in the 1842 Almanach as at Pavée-St. André 19, but it is doubtful if he did much binding, other than industrial, in which he was associated with his brother-in-law Engel, though J. Coulet's Cat. No. 29 of 1949 quotes a signed binding with his signature.

SCHELE   *? Paris*

Lesné '27, p. 375, refers to him as an excellent producer of gilders' small tools.

SCHENCKEL, Jean-Daniel   *Strassburg*

The Strohl Manuel for 1824 gives his address as Serruriers 19.

PLATE XX Lecrêne

187

SCHENCKEL, Th. *Strassburg*

An edge-marbler, operating in 1846 at Place St. Thomas 1 and Serruriers 12.

SCHERE-MARTIN *Paris*

Located at Trois-Pavillons 1 in 1842–43.

SCHMIDT *Paris*

Worked at Favart 3 in 1842–49.

SCHOEFFER, *Chrétien* *Strassburg*

The Mercure Alsacien for 1846 locates him at Miroir 4.

SCHULZE, C. A.

Romb. '47/C.555 mentions a Restoration binding by the above, but gives no indication of his place of operation.

SELLIER, *Pierre-Suzanne* *Paris*

Received in 1775 and lived at rue des Carmes; was at Charretière 16 in 1797, and at No. 17 in 1799. The cataloguer of the Whitney Hoff 1933 sales suggests that the Cellier Fils binding No. 670 may be by the above.

SENAC *Toulouse*

Was at rue Bouquières 19 between 1838–48.

SENEZ

Romb. '47/A.634 refers to a contemporary binding by the above on a work dated 1843.

SERLEYS *Lille*

At rue St. Etienne 15 in 1835.

SERRE (*and gilder*) *Paris*

Worked at St. Jacques 283 in 1803 and then from 1815 at No. 30. He is last noted in 1842 at Plâtre-St. Jacques 28. Sch. III, 227, has an illustration of his work in the later Empire style, and my own collection contains a 2-volume *Campagnes Memorables* of 1817 in decorative red morocco, with ticket.

PLATE XXI   Leteurtre

189

SERRE   *Amiens*

   At Orfèvres 11 in 1826.

SICARD   *Nantes*

   Addresses: rue Crébillon; ('04) ditto, Maison Barbier ('08); rue de la
   Fosse ('25 as Vetil-Sicard); and ('28 as Sicard).

SIMIER, *René (Père)*   *Paris*

   He is *not* mentioned in the 1797–98 Almanach. Tradition states that
   he left the army about 1798, and devoted himself to binding, and
   the 1847 Almanach refers to the firm as founded in 1800. Between
   1809–12 he appears to have been "Binder to the Empress Marie
   Louise", and in 1826 Simier "Père et Fils" are listed in the Almanach
   as "Binders to the King, Madame, and the Duc de Bordeaux". His
   appearances in the Almanachs seem to range from ('09–'26), when
   the entry becomes "Père et Fils". He possibly died shortly after ('26).
   He received a Medal of Honour in 1819, and he or his firm received
   various awards over the succeeding thirty years. His influence and
   position in Empire and Restoration binding are summarised in the
   Introduction. His variety and technique were superb; he had no
   superior and few rivals during his career. His work can be studied
   in most of the important Catalogues. His first known address in 1809
   seems to have been Neuve-des-Bons-Enfants 35, from whence he
   moved in 1814 to St. Honoré 152. Bér. Rel. I, p. 35, however, gives
   his address in 1810 as Passage Radziwill, which leads out of Neuve-
   des-Bons-Enfants to rue Valois.

SIMIER, *Alphonse (Fils)*   *Paris*

   He appears on his own in 1821 at Bertin-Poirée 6 in the 1821
   Almanach, and then in 1826 appears with his father at rue St. Honoré
   152, where he carried on the business under the family name after
   his father's death.

SIMIER, *(? Jean)*   *Paris*

   This binder, who appears in the 1847–49 Almanachs, is reputed to
   be a nephew of the elder Simier.

SIMON   *Paris*

   Noted in 1803 at Carmes 5.

PLATE XXII Lorilliard

SIMON   *Nantes*

Addresses: rue de Carmes ('29); rue des Bons Français ('33); rue Fénelon ('41–'45).

SIMON   *Paris*

In 1847 he is reported at St. Roumain 9.

SIMONET   *Toulouse*

At rue du Poids de l'Huile in 1807.

SINET   *Paris*

His address between 1847–49 was Mathurins 3.

SIX, *Alexandre*   *Lille*

From 1825–34 he worked at rue de l'A.B.C. 24 (or 20). His widow carried on the business from 1835–47.

SOLLER   *Paris*

Makes an appearance at Place Sorbonne 3 bis in 1847.

SOLLIER   *Nantes*

At rue Mercœur ('44); rue du Marchix 1 ('48).

SOMMERVOGEL, *Rosalie*   *Strassburg*

The Strohl Manuel for 1824 gives her address as Miroir 4.

SOMMIER, *Joachim*   *Lyons*

Worked at the following addresses: Raisin 31 ('10); 11 ('13); Grande rue Mercière 48 ('21); 57 ('42).

SOUDANAS   *Bordeaux*

At rue Porte-Dijeaux in 1824.

SOUDANAS, *Jean-Baptiste*   *Limoges*

First noted at rue Arbre-Peint in 1836, and then at rue Puy-Vieille-Monnaie in 1846.

PLATE XXIII Lunier-Belier

SOUDANAS, Léonard   *Limoges*

Master-binder in 1789.

SOUDANAS, Martial Aîné   *Limoges*

Master-binder 1788–89.

SOUDANAS-DESCHAMPS   *Limoges*

At rue de la Courtine between 1836–46.

SOULAS (or SOULE)   *Toulouse*

At rue du Collège Royal between 1837–48.

SOULIE   *Paris*

Between 1835–40 he functioned at Quai des Augustins 11.

SOUZE

SOYER   *Paris*

Noted at Harpe 35 in 1847.

SPACHMANN   *Paris*

The addresses given in the Almanachs are as follows: Coquenard 24 ('35); Neuve-des-Petits-Champs 19 ('38); Tournon 33 ('47–'49). The 1835 Almanach states that he also dealt in office equipment. There is no mention of him between ('38–'48). A binding by him seen in Brussels in mid-1949 was previous in date to 1838.

SPECH   *Paris*

Makes an appearance in 1842–43 at St. Jean-de-Beauvais 15.

SPECHEL, D.-Th.   *Strassburg*

Noted in 1846 at Hôpital 18.

SPEICH, F.   *Strassburg*

Was at Ste. Elisabeth 33 in 1846.

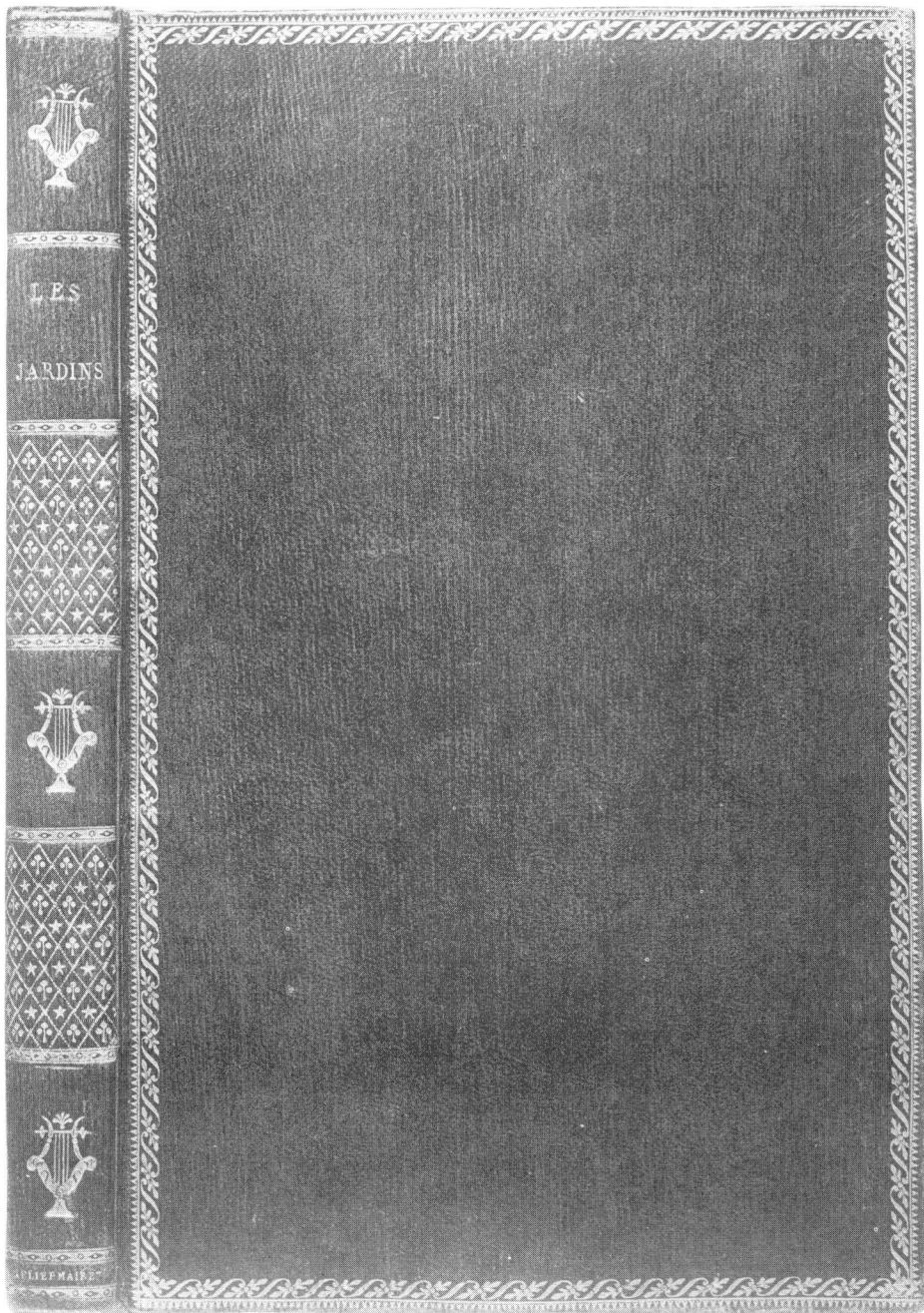

PLATE XXIV Mairet

195

STAEBLE

See Boerner XXI/177.

STAMM, Charles-Guillaume　　　　　　　　　　　　　　*Strassburg*

His address in 1824 was Grande rue de l'Eglise 2.

STRADEL, Jeune　　　　　　　　　　　　　　　　　　*Montauban*

Sch. III, 287, describes and illustrates a binding by this binder and
stationer living at rue Camirade. The binding appears to be contemporary with the book, i.e. 1821.

STRAUSSI　　　　　　　　　　　　　　　　　　　　　*Paris*

Noted in 1847 at Vieilles-Haudriettes 4.

STRUMIA　　　　　　　　　　　　　　　　　　　　　*Paris*

From 1836–47 he was active at St. Jean-de-Beauvais 18.

STUBER, Chrétien-Philippe　　　　　　　　　　　　　　*Strassburg*

Noted at Faubourg de Pierre 1 in 1824.

SUBRA　　　　　　　　　　　　　　　　　　　　　　*Paris*

At Cluny 1 in 1842.

SUPIE, Claude　　　　　　　　　　　　　　　　　　　*Lyons*

Worked at Grande rue Mercière 51 in 1810, and then at No. 64 from
1813–32.

SUSBIELIK　　　　　　　　　　　　　　　　　　　　*? Saintes*

Sch. II, 187, describes and illustrates a binding by the above which
can be safely ascribed to about 1800.

SUSSE　　　　　　　　　　　　　　　　　　　　　　*Paris*

This binder I have not been able to trace in the Almanachs. I have a
mosaic binding with his label, giving his address as Passage Panoramas 7/8, which can be dated with confidence about 1827.

PLATE XXV Mairet

SUSSE, *Frères* *Paris*

These binders, evidently connected with the previous entry, appear to have operated from 1839, when they received a "B" award, till 1849. Their address was Place Bourse 31 and Passage Panoramas 7/8.

TAFFOIREAU *Paris*

First noted at Sorbonne 12 in 1832 and then at Hautefeuille 14 from 1842–49.

TALLIADE, *Aîné* *Paris*

Describes himself as "pupil of Simier Père". Worked first at Bailleul 11 in 1836 and then at St. Honoré 94 from 1838–49.

TALLIADE, *Jeune* *Paris*

Started in 1836 at Dauphin 14 and then from 1838–42 worked at Boucheries St. Germain 16.

TALLNAUD (*or TALLUAND*) *Limoges*

Active at rue des Combes between 1836–46.

TAVEL

D. d'E. reports his signature in 1834 (see Cat. Wassermann, 1260).

TAVERNIER *Paris*

At Maçons 3 between 1847–49.

TEISSIER *Paris*

See *Tessier*.

TERTRE *Paris*

Appears in 1842 at Servandoni 11.

TENON, *André-Louis* *Lyons*

The Lyons Indicateur gives him first in 1810 at Thomassin 10 and then at No. 18 in 1813–16.

PLATE XXVI Martin

TERZUOLO
Paris

He is described on a label on a morocco binding on a musical MS. (about 1825–30) as "Papetier du Roi, Chaussée d'Antin, coin Neuve des Mathurins". It is not certain whether he was actually a binder himself.

TESSIER (*or TEISSIER*), N.
Paris

He succeeded J.-C.-H. Lemonnier about 1780, and used the former's label with appropriate alterations. He further varied his label all through the vicissitudes of the Revolution, the Empire, and the Restoration with remarkable cynicism and apparently undisturbed success. (See Gruel II, p. 164, for reproductions of these labels.) He does not figure in the 1797–98 Almanach, but thereafter consistently between 1803–43. It is hard to believe that it was the same individual, but the firm went on in rue La Harpe. The first address in 1780 was No. 165, then in 1803 No. 132, and from 1809 onwards to 1843 at No. 45. A binding dating about 1803 figures in my own collection.

TESSIER (*or TEISSIER*), *René*
Paris

Worked at the following addresses: Mont-St. Hilaire 10 ('03); No. 6 ('15); Cloître-St. Benoît 20 ('21).

TESSIER, *Aîné*
Paris

At St. Dominique 17 in 1843–47.

TESSIER
Paris

Appears at Sept-Voies 7 in 1843.

TEXIER
Bordeaux

At rue Judaique 11 in 1848.

TEYCHENEY
Bordeaux

At rue Esprit-des-Lois 19 in 1833.

THERON, P.
Paris

Noted in the Almanachs between 1832–42 at Quai-St. Michel 9. A binding by him is described and illustrated in Sch. III, 308.

PLATE XXVII   Meslant

THESSEL   *Paris*

    Resided at Harpe 105 in 1803.

THIEBLEMONT   *Paris*

    Noted in the 1803 Almanach at Pavée 4.

THIERRY   *Paris*

    Figures at St. Denis 309 in 1840–42.

THIESSE, *Jean-Benjamin*   *Paris*

    Received in 1772 and noted in the Almanachs at Place Cambrai 13
    (’97); 5–3 (’09).

THIRLET, *Charles-Jacques (and bookseller)*   *Metz*

    Born at Paris January 4, 1826. Came to Metz about 1847 and worked
    at rue de la Tête d’Or. Died January 8, 1884.

THOBOL   *Marseilles*

    At rue de l’Académie 3A in 1841–42.

THOMAS   *Paris*

    At St. Merri 7 in 1832.

THOMAS, *Jean-Baptiste*   *Limoges*

    Master-binder in 1789.

THOMAS, (? E.)   *Paris*

    First noted at Fouarre 19 in 1821, and later at Poterie 3 (1835–42).
    Lesné 27, p. 340, quotes him as little-known. Bér. Rel. I, p. 34,
    mentions a Thomas at rue St. Martin in 1814, who may be the same.

THOMPSON   *Paris*

    Only appears in the 1842 Almanach at Neuve Coquenard 18, but he
    bound well into the (’50s.)
    Maggs 661/75 and 172, illustrate examples of his work differing
    widely in date and style. He was very addicted to plain Jansenist
    bindings. His passion for book-collecting is said to have dissipated
    his earnings as a binder.

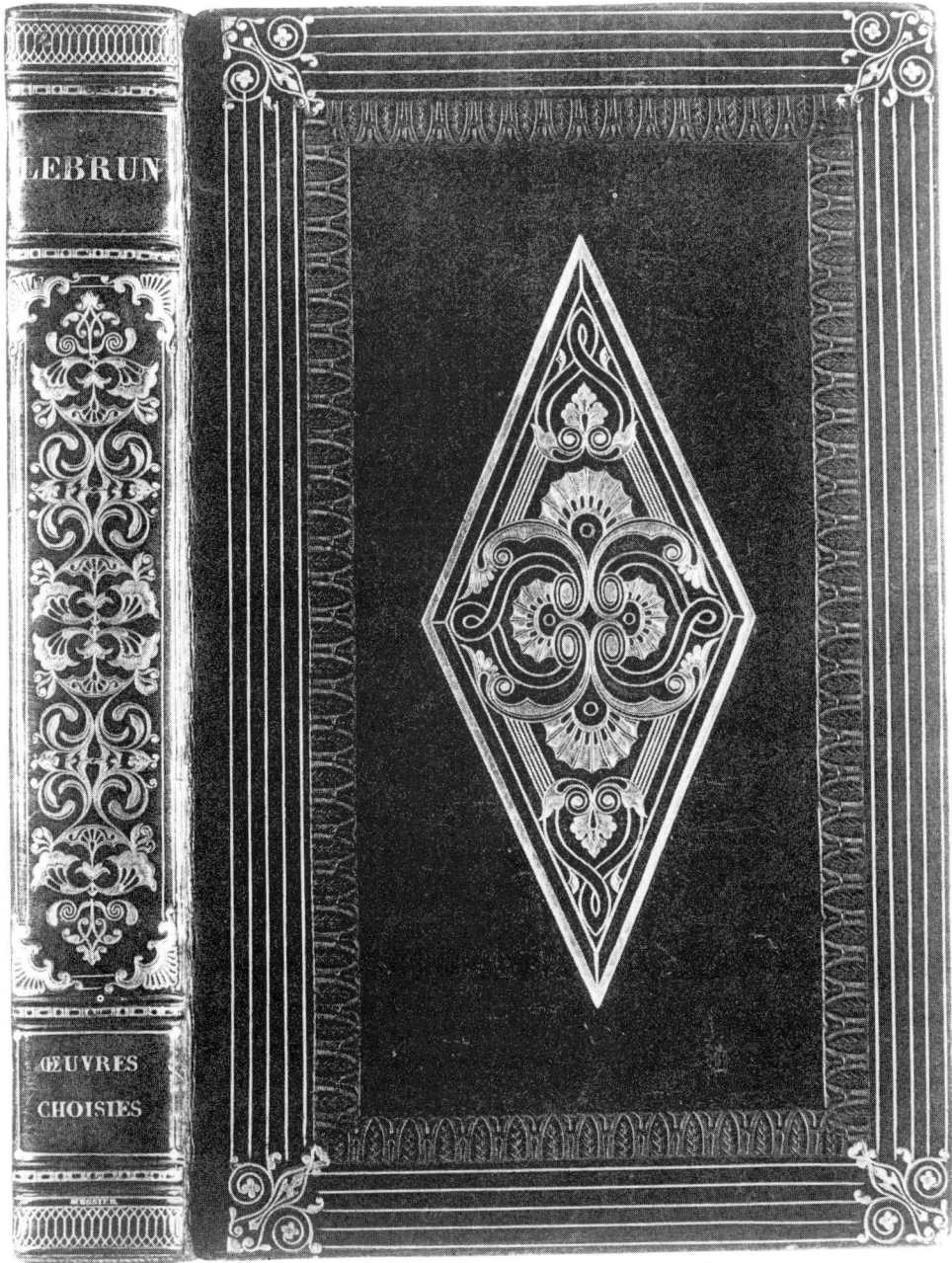

PLATE XXVIII Messier

203

THOMPSON and LARDIERE   *Paris*

This combination appears in the 1840–42 Almanachs with the address of Louis-le-Grand 30. The specimen illustrated in Sch. 329 falls well after our period.

THOUVENIN, Joseph (l'Aîné)   *Paris*

Born September 6, 1790, died January 9, 1834. Worked on his own from 1813–34.

Addresses: St. Jacques 75 ('13); Ecole de Médicine ('15); Fossés St. Victor 36 ('19); Mazarine 34 ('23); Mazarine 29 and Passage Dauphine 36 ('30).

Thouvenin Joseph, (l'Aîné) was the eldest of three brothers, the younger of whom, Joseph and François, are dealt with below. Most of the particulars here given as to Joseph are taken from the notice on "Les Thouvenins" published by Léon Gruel in the *Bulletin du Bibliophile et du Bibliothécaire*, Paris, 1898, pp. 435–46 and 508–14.

He started to work as odd boy with Bozérian Jeune in 1802, and according to his own account had acquired great competence by 1806. He set up on his own in 1813, apparently to learn the gilding which Bozérian Jeune had been unwilling to teach him. He admits that for many years later he was quite incapable of attaining the standard set by many English binders, notably Ch. Lewis, whose work was brought to him as models by his customers. Only by 1830 did he feel that he had obtained the necessary experience, and built up a team of binders which enabled him to compete successfully with all English binders of the epoch.

Thouvenin's heyday lasted only four years, for he died early in 1834, possibly as a result of blood-poisoning in the foot. In the interval he had achieved, in his new and excellently installed workshop in the Passage Dauphine, both a reputation as the leading binder of his epoch, and social connections which he evidently enjoyed and deserved. He was fully aware of the excellence and lasting workmanship of his bindings, which he did not hesitate to compare to their credit with the work of Bozérian Jeune who, he stated, had made a fortune by massacring all the books that had passed through his hands. Finally, his name has been immortalised by mentions in the pages of Balzac and Stendhal, and his connection with Charles Nodier has added a lustre to both their names, often inscribed on shields on the sides of books bound for and by them respectively.

PLATE XXIX   Monniot

THOUVENIN, J. Aîné et Cie. *Paris*

This business was founded in 1828 at rue Mazarine 34, and continued from 1830 at No. 29 and at Passage Dauphine 36 till about 1842. Its manager was M. Edouard Ray, and it was presumably founded to relieve Thouvenin of much of the financial and business routine with which he seems to have found difficulty in dealing. Complaints as to his slowness in delivering bindings have a familiar ring to-day. A price-list issued prior to 1830 appears in L. Gruel's article on "Les Thouvenins". (See *Thouvenin, (Joseph l'Aîné)*). Prices varied from 50 frs. for a full rich morocco folio to 1.25 frs. for a half-calf plain back in −18°.

THOUVENIN, Joseph, Jeune *Paris*

Brother of Joseph Thouvenin l'Aîné. Probably working as early as 1822, as he received an honourable mention in the Paris Exhibition of the following year. Figures in the Paris Almanach from 1826–36, first at rue de la Parcheminerie 2, and later from 1835 at rue de la Harpe 58. He died in 1844. He was an excellent binder in a slightly heavier style than his elder brother. Correspondence published by L. Gruel shows the extreme care he took over his tools and the finish of his bindings. A small *Pastor Fido* by Guarini in my own collection approximates to the best work of Charles Lewis.

THOUVENIN, François *Paris*

This third brother of the two well-known Joseph Thouvenins is stated to have worked at rue du Plâtre, though no authenticated specimen of his work seems to be known. He died of cholera in 1832.

THRANER, Charles-Jacques *Strassburg*

The Strohl Manuel of 1824 gives his address as Ste. Hélène 13. An example of his work is described, but not illustrated, in Sch. III, 292. A two-volume red morocco binding in my own collection on *Histoire de la Maison de Hesse* 1817 represents an extremely interesting survival of classical motives into Restoration times.

TIGER, Gabriel-Jean *Paris*

See Gruel I, p. 164. Received in 1748, and seems to have been still active in 1797–98 "au pilier littéraire", Place Cambrai.

PLATE XXX   Muller succ. Thouvenin

207

TIGER, *Christophe-Jean-Baptiste*   *Paris*

See Thoinan, p. 397. He was the son of Gabriel-Jean, and received in 1786. He was probably the same as the Tiger who figures in the 1797–98 Almanach at Place Cambrai 19.

TIGER, *Fils*   *Paris*

Appears in the 1803 Almanach at Place Cambrai 19, and was no doubt the son of C. J. B. Tiger.

TIGER, *Veuve*   *Paris*

Thoinan, p. 397, states that she also worked at Place Cambrai till 1804, but I have not been able to trace this in the Almanachs. The 1799 Almanach Typographique mentions her.

TINGREVILLE   *Paris*

Figures in 1847 at St. Nicolas d'Antin 59.

TIR

No particulars available.

TOUACHE   *Marseilles*

Worked 1841–48 at rue de la Palud 75, coin de la 3e Calade.

TOUBILLON, *François*   *Lyons*

The 1832 Lyons Indicateur gives his address as Ferrandière 13.

TOUPRIANT, (*et Cie.*, 1838)   *Paris*

First figures at Grange-Batelière 9 in 1838, and two years later at Provence 30.

TOURNADRE

D. d'E. reports a binding about 1844.

TRENSZ, J.   *Strassburg*

The Mercure Alsacien of 1846 gives his address at Grand'rue 23.

PLATE XXXI   Pralon

TREPAN   *Péronne*

His address in 1826–27 was: Sur la Place.

TRIBOUILH   *Bayonne*

Worked at Place Notre Dame about 1840–50.

TRIPIER-BRADEL, *Ch.*   *Paris*

Appears at Richelieu 68 in 1842, and next year at No. 8, when he styles himself "Binder of the Royal Library". Late in 1948 I saw a complete calf binding by him of the school prize type. He was still binding in 1849. A blind-stamped morocco album in my own collection (not later than 1845) bears a ticket "Ch. Tripier-Bradel/ Papetier Relieur/ 18 rue Richelieu".

TRIPON, *L.*

TROILON, *Pierre-Joseph*   *Lyons*

Makes a first appearance in 1821 at Ferrandière 12, and lastly in 1842 at Palais-Brillet 18.

TROTEBAS   *Marseilles*

Started at rue Couttellerie 23 in 1824, moved to No. 45 in ('31), and then from 1834–38 was at No. 28.

ULMAN   *Paris*

Mentioned in 1847 as a binder of prayer-books in velvet, operating at Chapon 1.

ULLMANN-HERZOG   *Paris*

First appears at Grands-Augustins 29 and St. André-des-Arts 6 in 1840, and subsequently in 1843 at Croix-des-Petits-Champs 52.

VABOIS   *Paris*

Working at Fossés St. Jacques 8 between 1838–42.

VABOIS, *Jeune (Alphonse)*   *Paris*

Followed his father at Fossés St. Jacques 8 from 1843–49. In the latter year he added the Christian name of "Alphonse".

PLATE XXXII Purgold

VABRE   *Toulouse*

   At rue Lafayette in 1837.

VABRE, Aîné   *Toulouse*

   At rue Rivals 1838–48.

VABRE, Veuve   *Toulouse*

   Mentioned in 1847 at rue de la Baruthe.

VALADE   *Limoges*

   Master-binder in 1789.

VALENCE   *Marseilles*

   Addresses: rue St. Ferréol ('12); rue Vacon ('13); rue St. Ferréol 13
   ('18); rue Venture 18 ('41–'48).

VALENTIN, François   *Paris*

   His addresses were as follows: Helder 12 and Taitbout 7 ('35);
   Caumartin 29 ('36) ;Neuve Coquenard 24 ('38–'49). My own collection
   contained a typical 2-volume binding on the Gigoux *Don Quichotte*, in a
   rather heavy rocaille style, and an effective Gothic binding in morocco
   of the "publisher's binding" type on *Galerie des Femmes de Walter
   Scott* 1840. Also worked with Boersch, *q.v.*

VANACKERE   *Lille*

   Working in rue Notre-Dame in 1788–89.

VANACKERE, Veuve   *Lille*

   Also worked in 1788–89 at rue des Tanneurs.

VANETTE   *Paris*

   Entitles himself as pupil of Bradel. The Almanachs give him as
   working at Froidmanteau (also called Fromental, or Fromanteau) 15,
   between 1826–32, though R.L.B. places his debut as early as 1810.
   Desc. II, 376, illustrates a binding in the black blind stamp style
   in which Meslant specialised. Sch. III, 302, is a very ordinary
   production.

PLATE XXXIII   Rondeau

213

VANNEHIN   *Lille*

Mentioned in the 1788–89 Lille Almanach at rue des Malades.

VARES   *Orleans*

Working at rue Bourgogne in 1807.

VARESY (sewer)   *Marseilles*

At rue de la Reynarde 5 in 1838.

VARLET   *Paris*

Thoinan, p. 400, states that he appears as early as 1800. I have traced
him in the Almanachs from 1803 at St. Jean-de-Beauvais 7, and then
at No. 13 ('09–'10).

VELLIO   *Marseilles*

At rue Haxo in 1803 and rue Vacon in 1805.

VENTE   *Paris*

He probably just comes into our period, being established in 1792
at rue des Anglais. A full account of his career can be found in
Thoinan, pp. 400–404.

VERGER   *Paris*

First worked in 1836 at Cluny 1, and later in 1847 at Marché Neuf 10.

VERGNE   *Limoges*

At rue du Collège in 1836.

VERNIER-REITZ

A late binder of our period.

VERPILLAT, Etienne   *Lyons*

The Lyons Indicateur for 1832 gives his address as Capucins 5.

VERREAUX, Simon   *Dijon*

Resided at rue Verrerie between 1823–33 and did cheap binding for
the Dijon Library.

PLATE XXXIV Rosa

215

VERZIER, *Joseph*   *Lyons*

Worked at Raisin 18 in 1810.

VESNAT   *Paris*

Noted at St. Jean-de-Beauvais 16 in the years 1847–49.

VETIL-SICARD   *Nantes*

See *Sicard*.

VIALARD (*and restorer*)   *Paris*

Worked for years at Collège d'Harcourt from 1803 onwards, and makes a last appearance in 1826 at Contrescarpe St. Marcel 21.

VIE, *Veuve*   *Paris*

Appears at Montagne-Ste. Geneviève 54 in 1847.

VIENER, L.   *Nancy*

Known from the very ordinary binding described and illustrated in Sch. III, 291.

VIGNEAUD

A binding dating about 1825 seen at Stock's, Paris, December 1949.

VILLENEUVE   *Nantes*

At Place St. Vincent in 1841.

VINCENS, *Père et Fils*   *Toulouse*

These excellent provincial binders, who appear to have worked between 1818–30, had their address at rue d'Astorg 10. I have an excellent specimen in a full blue morocco binding with the arms of Charles X on the 1829 *Jeux Floraux*. Another fine example is described and illustrated in Sch. III, No. 311. The father seems to have worked at Cours St. Rome as early as 1807, and a firm of Vincens Frères existed in 1847 at rue d'Astorg 22.

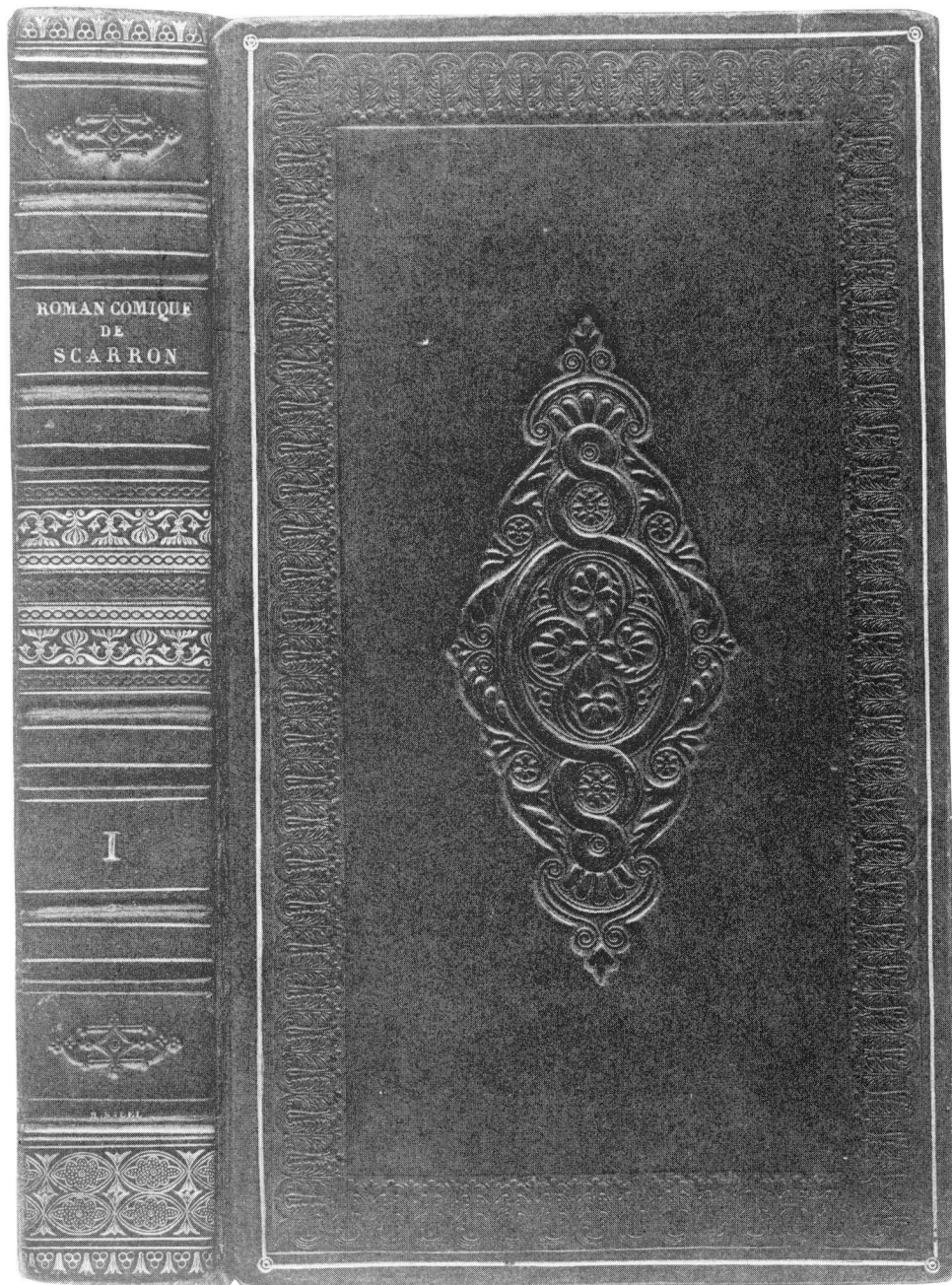

PLATE XXXV   H. Salel

217

VINET   *Paris*

Worked at rue du Roule 15, and received an honourable mention in the 1827 Exhibition. (See *Dècle.*)

VINOT   *Limoges*

At rue du Temple in 1836 and at rue du Collège in 1846.

VINSAC   *Bordeaux*

Addresses: rue des Bahutiers ('89–'92); rue des Trois-Conils ('07); rue Traversière, près la rue Beaufleuri ('11).

VITALIS   *Paris*

Quoted in the 1842 Almanach at Montmartre 20.

VITALIS, Jeune (music-binder and gilder)   *Paris*

Noted in 1843 at Tiquetonne 8.

VIVET, Ed.   *Paris*

Makes no appearance in the Almanachs, but may well have worked from 1820 to about 1850.

VOGEL, E.   *Paris*

The facts that we know of him are scanty, though Bér. Rel. I, p. 34, mentions that he was already working in 1814. He first appears in the Almanachs in 1826, at rue Dauphine 24, and then from 1832 onwards till 1849 at Four-St. Germain 78. It is hardly worth while quoting examples of his work, of which Desc. II shows thirty examples. His work is so closely akin to that of Thouvenin that there seems little doubt that they must, at some stage, have worked together. Vogel seems to have been capable of doing all Thouvenin's work, except the really first-line productions. Vogel was definitely at the top of the second class.

VUITON   *Lyons*

Quoted by the 1842 Lyons Indicateur.

PLATE XXXVI   Thraner

WADOUX   *Boulogne*

Recorded in the 1845–46 Boulogne Annuaire as a binder and stationer
working at Réligieuses Anglaises 10. An example of his work is to
be found in the Boulogne Mun. Library, C.2065.

WAGNER, G.   *Paris*

Béraldi Rel. II, p. 54, states that Engel worked with Wagner before
setting up with Schaeck in 1838. He appears in the Almanachs for
the first time in 1840 at Passage de l'Industrie 10, and later at Poupée
9 in 1847. Rauch Cat. No. 1, No. 329, illustrates a binding by G.
Wagner on Heine's *Buch der Lieder*, which may be an early production of this binder, and I have a fine cathedral specimen in my own
collection.

WAGUENER   *Paris*

Appears at Vieille-Boucherie 24 in 1842, and in the following year
at Poupée 20.

WAHL   *Paris*

Worked at Ecosse 6 from 1832–47. He apparently specialised in
artistic repairs needing the employ of adhesives, such as remounting,
etc.

WAHL, R.   *Paris*

Noted at Boulevard des Italiens in 1842.

WEDDING   *Angoulême*

The binding illustrated and described in Sch. III, 274, gives his
address as rue Ste. Marie. It is a provincial binding, about ten years
behind the equivalent Parisian binding.

WEIDLE

He is known to me from a three-quarter green morocco binding in
my own collection, which I should place about 1825–30. I suspect
that it is Belgian.

WIENER

Known to me only from a signed half-calf binding in my own
collection on Tschokke's *Histoire Suisse*, 2 vol., 1828.

PLATE XXXVII Wagner

221

WIGNAN *Lille*

Quoted in the 1788–89 Lille Almanach at rue des Malades.

WYNANTS *Paris*

Cimetière-St. André 10 ('36) and Poupée 5 ('40–'42).

YSABEAU *Paris*

From 1826–43 worked at Pont-de-Lodi 5. I have a fine full morocco binding by him dating about 1828 with curious deep channel effects on the back.

ZABERN *Strassburg*

This binder's name is to be found on a half-calf binding of the original edition of Lamartone's *Jocelyn*, 2 vol., 1836, seen at Evert's shop in Paris, February 1950. See also *Hering, G.*

ZAMEFING *Paris*

The Almanachs 1816–21 give his address as Ecosse 6.

ZEZZIO *Paris*

This binder worked for forty-five years, but I have never seen an example of his work. His addresses were: Carmes 26 ('97); St. Jacques 667 ('03); Foin-St. Jacques 15 ('09); Plâtre-St. Jacques 24 ('26); Bernardins 22 ('32–'42). The specimen described and illustrated in Sch. II, 160, has the Foin-St. Jacques label, and is in the late Derôme tradition. Another is described in Rosenthal's Cat. 20, No. 96, and appears to be of about the same date, though more elaborate in style. To date I have no idea of his Restoration work.

ZOUBRE *Paris*

Noted at St. Jacques 140 between 1847–49.

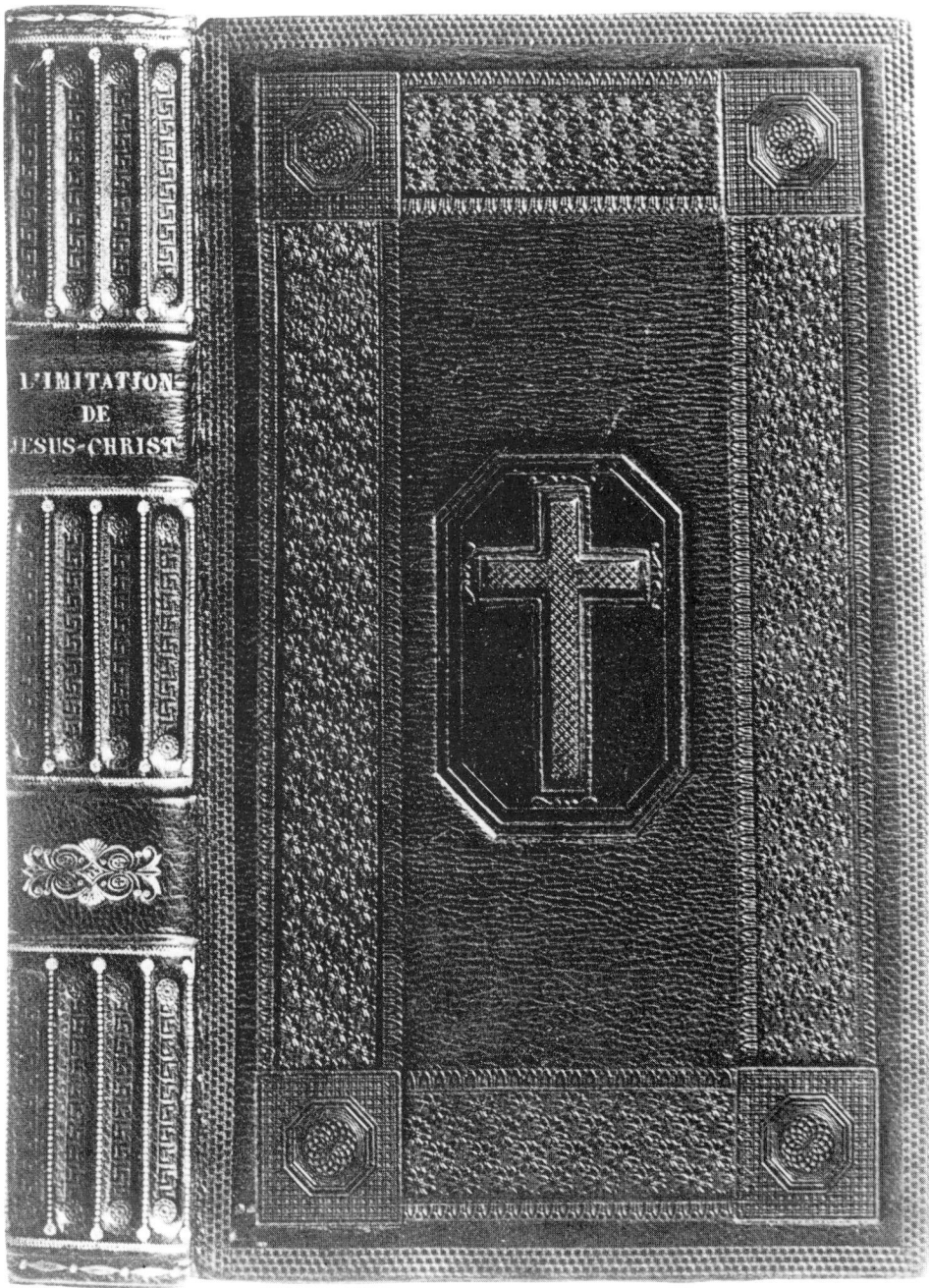

PLATE XXXVIII   Ysabeau

223

ADDENDA

While this work has been in the printer's hands, certain additional information has come to my notice, which I give below. The reference "D. de V. Cat." refers to the 2 volume catalogue of H.R.H. the Duc de Vendôme's sale which took place in Paris 1931–32.

ARNAUDE   *Bordeaux*

He seems to have worked between 1843–48 (see D. de V. Cat. No. 719).

BERVILLE   *Paris*

The only specimen known to me of this binder is mentioned and illustrated in D. de V. Cat. No. 1195. It appears to be fine work.

BOEGNER   *Paris*

See also A. Poursin's Cat. 223 No. 507.

BRAND   *Geneva*

Kundig's Cat. 95 Nos. 482 and 495, and Cat. 101 No. 487 leave no doubt that he was a Geneva binder.

BREAUTE

Mentioned in D. de V. Cat. No. 89. The bindings are described as romantic.

CASSASSUS

The question as to where this binder worked is further complicated by the fact that D. d'E. reports that the Belgian Almanach du Commerce states that a binder of the name was working in 1851 at No. 13 rue de l'Empereur, Brussels.

CHRETIEN   *Bordeaux*

Appears to have worked about the end of our period (see D. de V. Cat. No. 719).

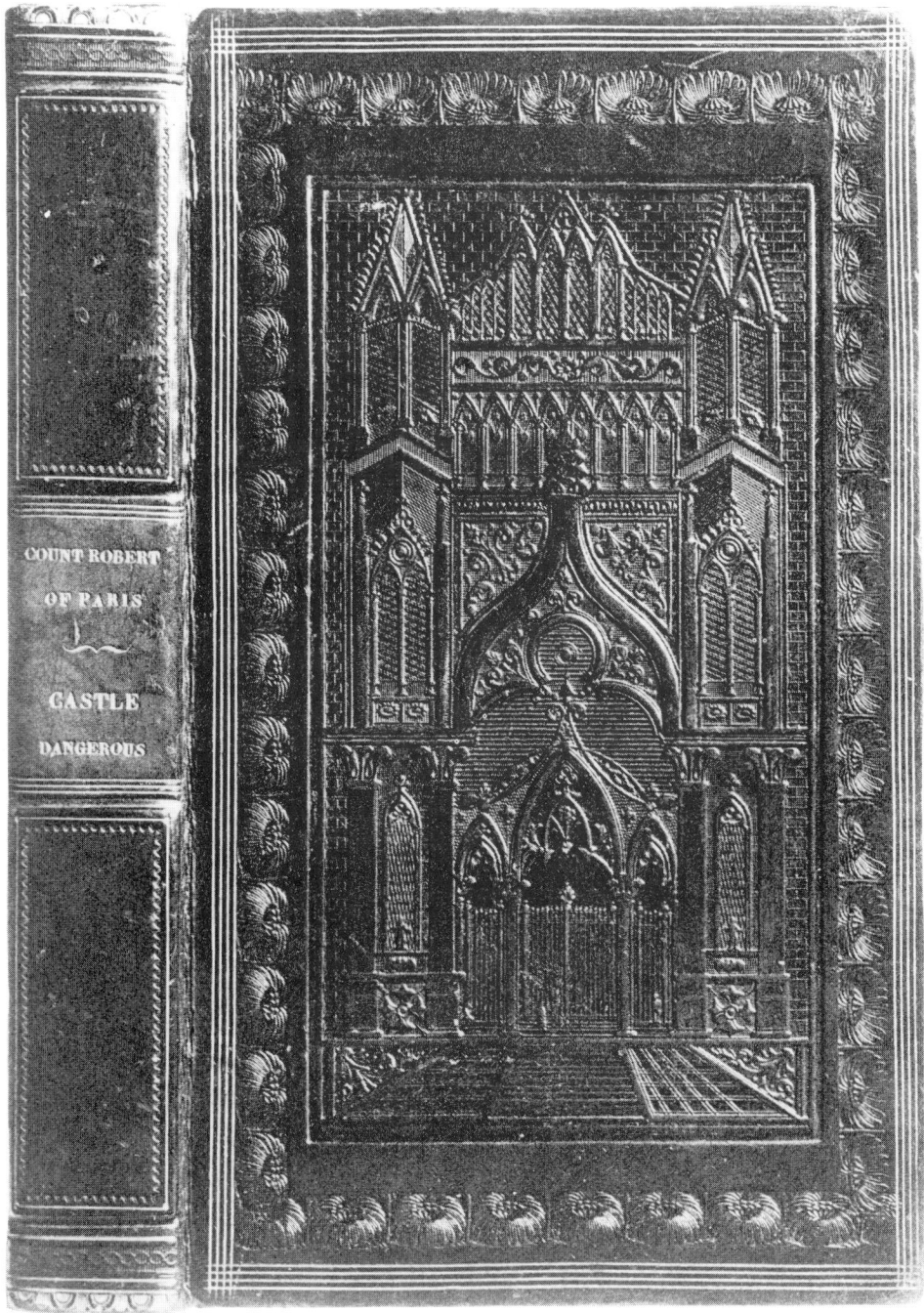

PLATE XXXIX Anon.

225

COMELARAN   *Paris*

   The D. de V. Cat. No. 372 shows that he was still working as late
   as 1844.

CORFMAT

   No. 1091 of the D. de V. Cat. appears to suggest that one of the
   family was working about 1833, possibly in Belgium.

DELRIEU   *Pau*

   Appears to have worked about 1838 (see D. de V. Cat. No. 95 and
   Kundig Cat. 101. No. 572).

HERSENT

   See also D. de V. Cat. No. 260.

LASALLE   *Paris*

   See also D. de V. Cat. 308 from which he may have been working
   well before 1840.

LE GALL

   Mentioned as the binder of No. 132 in the D. de V. Cat. Probably
   working about 1843.

LENDER

   Two bindings by this hitherto unknown binder are recorded in the
   D. de V. Cat. Nos. 1137/38.

MASSON   *Paris*

   I have seen his signature on a calf-bound copy of de Musset's
   Nouvelles, dated 1841.

OGINSKI, *Prince G.*   *Paris*

   He appears to have enjoyed some favour as a binder to the Royal
   Family during the reign of King Louis Philippe (see D. de V. Cat.
   passim).

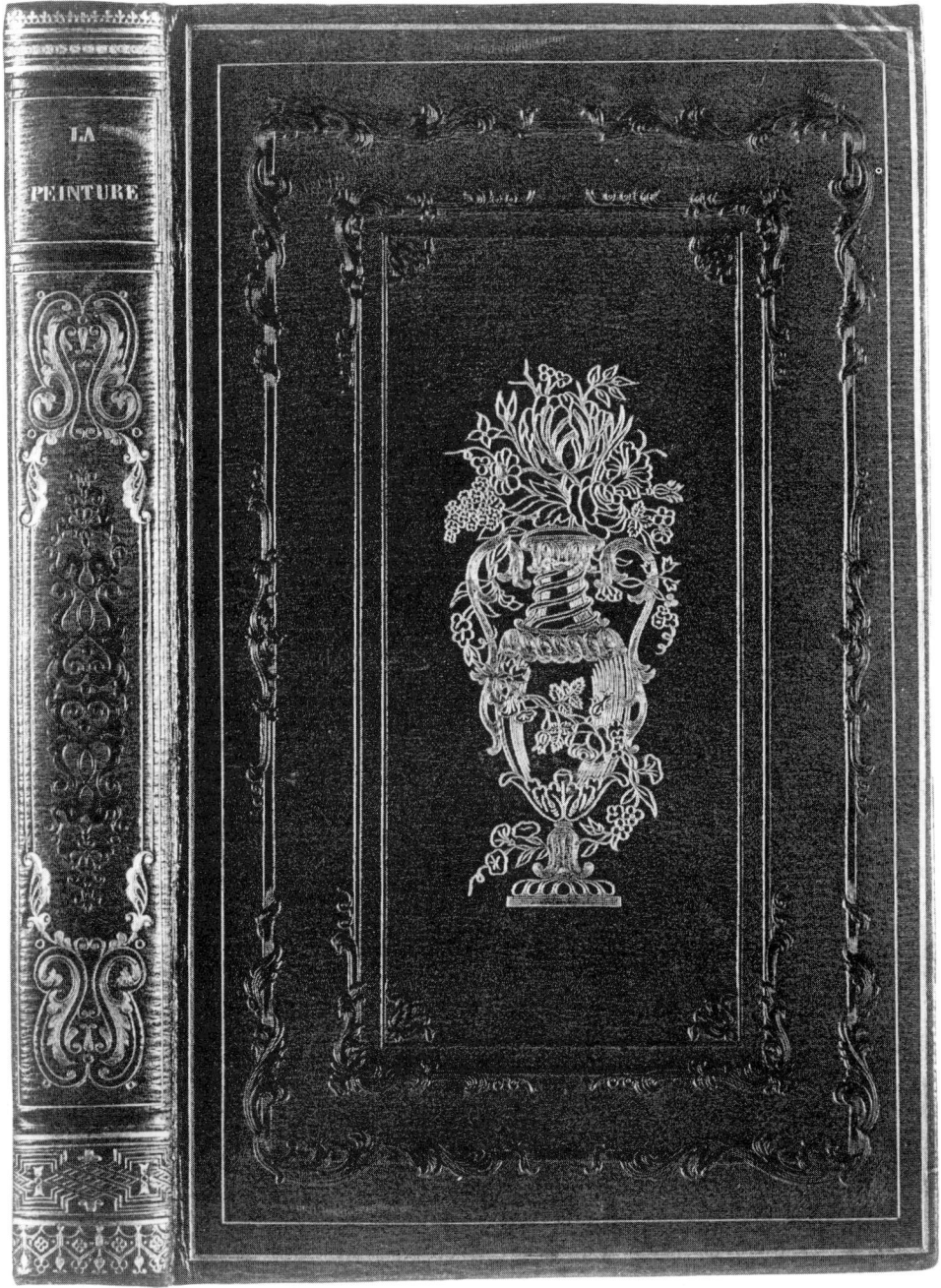

PLATE XL Anon.

PECLET

See D. de V. Cat. No. 211. He is doubtfully of our period.

SALEL, H.

I have a signed calf binding by him on a 2 volume Scarron: *Roman Comique*, dated 1825. See also D. de V. Cat. No. 410 where the binder's name is given as H. Saley.

TOURNADRE

D. d'E. reports a binding about 1844. (See also A. Poursin's Cat. 223, No. 297.)

WAGNER   *Paris*

I now have a binding in my own collection on a volume dated 1831, which appears to be contemporary.

ZEZZIO   *Paris*

An example of his restoration work is mentioned in D. de V. Cat. No. 1116.